COCOONS *of* SILK

A True Romance from 1930s China

Ping-Nan Yang

Translated by
Paul J.C. Yang & Dori Jones Yang

Cocoons of Silk: A True Romance from the 1930s China

Published by
East West Insights
www.eastwestinsights.com

Book cover design by Kathy Campbell
Book cover copyright © Dori Jones Yang
Printed in the United States of America.

ISBN-10: 0983527229
ISBN-13: 978-0-9835272-2-0
Library of Congress Control Number: 2012943685
East West Insights, Newcastle, WA

TABLE OF CONTENTS

Part I

YOUTHFUL
INDISCRETIONS

Xinpu Lianyungang
Haizhou Nancheng
Donghai Banpu
Guanyun Yangjiaji
Xiangshuikou

Funing

Yellow Sea

Xinghua

JIANGSU PROVINCE

Yangzhou

Zhenjiang Yangtze River

Nanjing

Changshu

Suzhou Shanghai

In Retrospect

The wintry wind blows harsh; rain soaks the city.
I awake in a strange place, not knowing where I am.
Looking back over the events of the last forty years
Half the memories are lost; only a trace remains.

Chapter One

PRECOCIOUS BOY

I WAS BORN AND GREW UP in a small town in eastern China called Nancheng, "South City." It is slightly inland from the harbor of Lianyungang, "Necklace of Clouds Harbor," in northern Jiangsu Province, on the coast halfway between Shanghai and Beijing. Lianyungang is known in China as the beginning of a major east-west railway that goes deep into the heart of the country and as a port for shipment of goods into and out of China. In Chinese literature, it is famous as the site of "Flower and Fruit Mountain," birthplace of the legendary Monkey King in the mythical classic *Journey to the West*.

Just three years after my birth, the last Emperor of China was overthrown. With the fall of the Qing (Ching)

Dynasty in 1911, thousands of years of Chinese imperial history abruptly ended. The Republic of China was formed under the leadership of Sun Yat-Sen. But during the 1910s and 1920s, China became increasingly chaotic because the central government was not strong enough to exert control over the whole country. It was an era of famines, bandits, and warlords.

Since I was born in the Year of the Monkey, my grandmother was convinced I would get myself into trouble when I grew up. So when I was three years old, she sent me to a Buddhist temple in the Western Hills and made me an 'absentee monk.' I did not have to live at the monastery, but she registered my name there. Her idea was to ask the Buddha to control me. From the time I was six years old, every year I had to put on Buddhist robes, beat on a small wooden knocker, and follow older monks to go to every household in the neighborhood asking for donations. This way I could help the old monks get money and food. Often when I did this, a group of boys would follow us and taunt me. I found this mockery painful.

My family was comfortable and middle-class, but when I was in elementary school our economic situation took a turn for the worse. We lived mainly on borrowed money, and my parents had to pawn a lot of property. The main reason for this was that my father was not a good businessman, although he always aspired to be one. He simply could not make a living. He borrowed money at high interest to do business. He opened a fabric shop, a

Chinese medicine shop, and even a store selling cooking oil. Every time, he wound up losing everything he had earned. Often he had to borrow even more money to pay for his debts, or else sell land he had inherited from his family. Our household net worth decreased every year, and our debts mounted higher and higher. Toward the end of each year, many creditors came to our house with little lanterns and sat in our living room, demanding they be repaid. Even until today, every time I see these little lanterns, it makes me nervous.

Sometimes we had difficulty getting enough to eat. At one point it was so bad we could afford to eat only cheap cornmeal and thin bread made of beans. Sometimes all we could eat was sweet potato leaves. Often I would go to bed hungry and couldn't sleep. My mother would come over to check on me and ask, "Are you hungry?" When I raised my head, I could see that my mother was crying. So when I was a boy, I hated creditors, businessmen, and people who ate rice – in other words, people who were well off.

During these tough years, my mother gave birth to many babies who died. In fact, I had eight younger sisters, and only one lived to adulthood. I especially remember a set of twins. One got sick, and my mother was tending to her in another room. I held the other twin and played with her. She seemed lively and healthy. The sick twin died, and within twenty-four hours the healthy one got sick and died, too. We were constantly mourning the loss of these little sisters.

Among my classmates, all the boys from merchant families automatically were my enemies. I fought them. The boys from poor families were on my side. I was the leader of that group. We always won. Once I got into a fight with a kid and broke his head. As it happened, his parents were Christians. They went to the school principal after that incident, and a foreign missionary came to our school and talked to the principal. I was severely punished. My father had to go to the church and set off a string of firecrackers to show his apology. From that time on, I added to my list one more category of people I despised: Christians.

During those days, strict Confucian family rules were being challenged, and many young people in China wanted to learn modern ways from the West. My parents were raised with traditional values, but my generation rebelled and wanted to build a new, modern China. We were quick to discard the old moral teachings but did not have a clear set of values to replace them. This was the cause of most of the traumas of my life as a young man.

In those days, businessmen were looked down on. The most respected men were highly educated government officials. All parents wanted their sons to be educated so they could get prestigious and lucrative positions in the government. Before my generation, wealthy families hired tutors to educate their sons at home. Schools were relatively new, and so was the education of girls.

From my earliest days, I had a romantic nature. In third grade, I fell in love with my cousin, Wu Xiulian. I look back on this as a sweet romance of innocent children, what we call "qingmei, zhuma" – tender plum-blossom, bamboo horse. We played together. When we were about ten years old, we privately promised to get married when we grew up. My parents seemed to like this idea, and so did hers. But my grandmother objected vigorously. Why? Because that cousin was the daughter of a concubine. To my grandmother, that was unacceptable. We two children sometimes held each other and cried, not knowing what to do.

After that, I fought less. When I finished fourth grade, I was ranked first in my class. A prominent elderly relative, Mr. Yang Jingshan, who had formerly served as a secretary for Sun Yat-Sen, happened to come back to his native town to pay respects to his ancestors, and he heard that I did very well at school. He invited me to dinner at his house, where he gave me a test. He asked me to give him matching words for each of four words: "Family, Tradition, Four Virtues."

I answered: "Wealth, Knowledge, Five Vehicles." This was a kind of intellectual poetic word-game scholars used to hone their literary talents.

The old man was impressed. He told my father, "This boy is gifted. We should nurture him. He shouldn't stay in elementary school any more. Have him take the exam for the No. 8 Teacher-Training High School."

My parents were very worried about the idea of having me leave home at such a young age. I also didn't want to go – primarily because I wouldn't be able to see my beloved cousin. But because this idea was suggested by the elderly Mr. Yang, who was highly revered in the whole city, nobody could say no.

On the day of the exam, my uncle took me to the site. The school official in charge asked me: "How old are you?" I told him I had just finished fourth grade. By Chinese reckoning, I was considered ten years old, although that is the age of nine by Western standards. He shook his head and patted me on the head.

One month after I took the exam, I received notice saying that I was admitted.

My father and uncle were very excited, but my mother cried. She was worried about me getting into fights and kicking off my covers at night.

I rushed to tell my cousin. She cried uncontrollably. She grabbed me, and her tears fell on my neck. She said, "Don't go. If you go, I don't want to live."

At that moment, her father walked in, holding a water pipe. He asked: "Why are you crying? Did you two fight again?"

So we rushed off. We ran to the East Hill, where there were no other people. We held each other and cried very hard. I promised I would write a diary for her every day; I also promised I would spend time with her every Saturday and Sunday when I came back home, and also during the summer and winter holidays. I also told her, "After five years, when I graduate from that school, I can be a teacher. Then we can get married. I will be able to afford to buy you pretty clothes and earrings."

We kept on talking and then we began to laugh. We stayed there from noon to sundown. She felt like a little kitten; I held her close to me. After it became dark and the dogs began to bark in the wilderness, we rushed home.

When I arrived at the No. 8 Teacher-Training School, two things bothered me right away. First, we had to shave our heads. Afterwards, I looked into the mirror, and I looked terrible. I thought: if my cousin sees me like this, she'll cry again. Second, all my classmates were a lot older than I was. I doubted I could possibly have anything in common with them.

But a lot of them liked to talk to me. One was named Gu Xiping. Many years later, after I came back to Nanjing from Xi'an, I found out that Gu had become a high official: head of the civil affairs department of Jiangsu Province. He was the one who got me a job as county executive in Changshu. But back in our school days, he looked like a country bumpkin. At that time, he told me he had a very pretty wife and two sons. Another classmate, with a beard, said his grandson was one year younger than I was.

The first class I went to was for composition. The teacher gave us a topic: "Your thoughts about shaving your head." I was the first to turn in my paper because I just wrote a poem:

When you cut off your hair,
Each hair you cut saddens you.
When you shave your head,
That doesn't mean you believe in Buddhism.
Now, no matter how frustrated I am by family
or national affairs
It cannot make me so angry
that my hair will stand on end.
Nothing will push off my hat.

(Note: In Chinese, this is in the perfect form of a classical poem, using clever rhymes and parallel words.)

The next day, the Chinese teacher, Mr. Jia, looked me up. He was a college graduate from Wuhan, very young. He liked me very much. He offered to teach me more about poetry if I would go to his dorm room every Tuesday and Thursday evening. I made a lot of progress in a very short time because he was an excellent teacher.

Although I was the youngest in the class, I was ranked first in all the courses I took – Chinese, English, math, music, and biology. The older boys were jealous. In addition to my classes, I picked up other interests, including playing drum, flute and organ, and I learned to sing kunqu, an ancient type of Jiangsu opera using famous poems as lyrics. When I first signed up for kunqu classes, where we learned to sing and memorized lyrics, there were fifty people. After two years, there were only five left in the class, and I was always Number One.

My uncle, my father's younger brother, was teaching at the elementary school associated with the Teacher-Training School. The following year, he went to Nanjing and entered the College of Hydraulic Engineering. But during my first year, he came to visit me every other day, to check on my studies and to see if I was homesick. He was not happy to find out I was studying kunqu. He told me not to be too serious about it because I could never make a living out of it. Later, though, this musical training did help me make a living, for quite a few years.

The year before I graduated from the No. 8 Teacher-Training School, when I was 15, my grandmother made the decision that I should marry. She found a wife for me, an illiterate woman who was about 20 years old. That woman seemed really old to me, and I had nothing in common with her. I vigorously opposed the whole idea of arranged marriage, which seemed hopelessly old-fashioned.

But I had no choice. On the day of the wedding, my father had to come to school and force me to go home to marry that illiterate woman. She and I slept together only once, and otherwise we lived apart. I always slept in the study on the western side of our house. Still, she got pregnant from that one encounter.

My first daughter, Huiling, came to this world from that unhappy union.

Chapter Two

FRUSTRATIONS OF A
YOUNG TEACHER

IN 1922, I GRADUATED from the No. 8 Teacher-Training School. At that time, my great uncle was the principal of the Donghai Provincial Middle School. He was my grandfather's brother; I called him Santaiye, meaning 'number three great uncle.' After my graduation, he gave me a recommendation to become a teacher at the elementary school associated with No. 8 Teacher-Training School. At that time, the teachers at that elementary school were making 60 yuan per month. Most teachers at other elementary schools earned a salary of only 20 yuan. But the principal of the No. 8 Teacher-Training School Elementary School, Mr. Xia, refused to hire me because he felt I was too young to be a teacher.

After the principal of No. 8 Teacher-Training School found out that I had an impeccable record in high school, he recommended that I should go on to study at Beijing University. The problem was, at that time, there was no way my family could pay for tuition and travel expenses to go to Beijing. Therefore, I had to give up the idea. I never blamed my father for this, because I knew he was very poor at the time. However, in the future this caused me to always save enough money for the education of my own children.

After graduation, I tried to land a job to support my family, which was very poor at the time. Finally two months later, I was hired as a substitute teacher at a local elementary school in Lianyungang. The principal's name was Liu. He always called me Xiao Yang, Little Yang. The first month I got paid my salary of 20 yuan, I bought a pair of earrings for my mother. She was so happy she cried. Some neighbors came over to see those earrings. Years later, in 1946, when my mother came to Xi'an to live with us, I noticed she was wearing those earrings.

Two months after I started teaching there, on a Sunday morning, several colleagues and I were walking around an old Buddhist temple near the school. We saw several nuns coming out of the temple. They were very polite to us. One of them was very young. She said she recognized me. She said her family name was Hu, my mother's family name. We were distant relatives. She said, "When you were in first grade, I was in fourth grade. Afterwards, because my family wanted to sell me to a salt merchant, I ran away from home and joined the nunnery." She was very emotional and started to cry. I felt very sorry for her. I said a few words to comfort her and then left.

Three days later, unexpectedly, she came to my school with an older nun to look for me. We talked in the school conference room a little while. Then they left. That evening, the principal called me to his office, very angry, and said, "Xiao Yang, I'm going to fire you. I never saw any teacher try to make friends with a nun." I was so angry I didn't even wait until he finished his statement. I went back to my room and picked up my things and went home. When I got home, it was after midnight. I told my parents the whole story. They didn't criticize me. My mother said, "I remember that girl. I feel really sorry for her. She has had such a terrible fate."

Within a few days, there were a lot of rumors around town. Some people said the Yang family was in deep trouble. They had never heard of anyone going to the monastery to flirt with a nun, and they thought I deserved to be fired. I had a distant cousin who often behaved badly and had been criticized by my father a few times in the past. During those rough days, he came to our house and pointed his finger at my father, saying, "You said I was bad. I haven't been so bad as to try to pick up a nun in a monastery." My father felt awful. I felt ashamed of the problem I had caused my parents.

Many years later, about 1948, I was the county executive in Changshu at a time when the area around Lianyungang was very chaotic because of the Communists. A lot of refugees came down from the North. At one point, I took in about three hundred refugees at once from my hometown region. Among the people who asked for my help were the principal who fired me, Mr. Liu, and that distant cousin. I denounced them, refused to accept them and turned them away.

During the rocky time of this scandal, Huiling was born. In retrospect, I think the reason she had such a harsh life was that she was born in an inauspicious time and place.

After the New Year, things seemed to turn around. In the spring of 1923, one of my distant uncles on my mother's side became the principal of an elementary school in Nancheng, called Kaiming Elementary. He hired me to teach English and music. I taught sixth grade English and also every week I taught one hour of English grammar. It didn't take long before I became well-known as a good teacher. Now I don't even remember what I taught – I can't speak a word English! It's funny. Later, I even taught English grammar at the junior high school level.

My favorite class was music. Other than teaching various types of common music, I also taught some of the basics of kunqu, the local style of opera. I even translated kunqu into written music, using numbers. The students loved it. (Kunqu started in Jiangsu, near Shanghai. It's a cross between folk songs and Peking opera. It is considered classical. Scholars like it because it adopted the style of Song dynasty lyric poetry.) Before long, the neighboring schools heard about it and sent teachers to find out what I was doing and try to copy it.

In 1924, the richest family in Nancheng, headed by a man named Wu Menghuan, hired me as a tutor for their son, to teach him English. They gave me 30 yuan a month. So, with the 20 yuan I got from school, I earned 50 yuan per month. At that time, our family life became very much easier. Plus, using the money I earned, I managed to buy back some of the land my father had lost. This made me very happy. Also, my grandmother had died by then. Therefore, the entire atmosphere at our home was much happier. I normally lived at the school even during winter and summer vacations, but I always came home for dinner. After dinner, I often held my baby daughter, Huiling, and played with her. She was a lovely little girl.

On Sundays and holidays, I often got together with my buddies from elementary school. We'd go to the countryside for hiking and swimming in a little river. Sometimes we would dig up sweet potatoes from a farm. We had a wonderful time.

This describes my life all the way till the summer of 1926. Then the principal of Guanyun County Middle/High School, a man named Mr. Wang, personally came to see me and ask me to teach in his school. My assignment was to teach music for the whole school. I also taught eighth grade (second year middle school) English. When this news became known throughout the town, everybody in Nancheng was envious because I had such a good job. My father rushed to get incense and offer it to our ancestors' graves to thank them for such good fortune and honor. My mother wanted to get me a new scholar's gown, a changshan, made of silk. My father disagreed, saying it would not be appropriate for a young man to wear silk. Regular cotton should be good enough.

It seems that whenever things are going well, something unpleasant happens. At this time, my cousin Wu Xiulian was about to get married. She was from a prominent family, so this became a major event in the town. Everybody seemed to be talking about it, but I felt very sad. I was anxious to see her one more time before her marriage. I couldn't think of anything else. Several times, I went to her house to see her. But I was always turned away at the door. That was frustrating.

On the night before her wedding, I decided to try one last time. I went to her family's big compound. A female servant answered the door and told me quietly, "Go to the back door right away." I went around to the back door. My heart was pounding. After a little while, the door opened. It wasn't my cousin. It was her mother. I wept and called her "jiuma," aunt. She grabbed me also, and her tears ran down her cheeks.

She said, "For the last several days, your cousin has refused to eat or sleep. She doesn't want to speak. She doesn't want to marry this man. If you see her now, you'll just make things worse. Don't you understand why this is a bad time to see her? If you insist on seeing her, she will die."

This aunt was from Changshu. My uncle, who was very rich, often went to the south, and during one of his trips, he picked her up and brought her home to be his concubine. To me, she was very nice, always diplomatic and easy-going and smart. After a few words, she persuaded me to go away without seeing my cousin. She touched my hair and used her sleeves to wipe my tears. She said, "Go home. Don't be foolish. Your cousin will always remember you."

After returning to my room at the school, I started to write a story about my love for my cousin. I poured out all my feelings and ranted about the hazards of not being able to choose your own marriage partner. After that, I wrote a long poem, using plain language, not in the rigid old classical style. After the May 4th movement of 1919, this kind of writing had become popular.

A week later, I sent that story and poem to the local newspaper, and after another week it was returned. This was the first time I submitted my writing to a newspaper – and also my first rejection letter. I felt really hurt. But I discovered that I felt better when I expressed my frustrations through writing. Soon after that, a friend recommended I send the story to a newspaper in Zhenjiang, a big city in the southern part of our province. It was finally published in the evening paper there. That was my first time in print.

Chapter Three

CAUGHT IN A
SILKWORM'S THREADS

WHEN I BEGAN TO TEACH at the county middle school, I was not yet twenty. Some of my students were older than I was. One of my students was Wu Youxia, who became a lifelong friend; he was actually a few years younger. I was nervous.

The first class I taught was ninth grade (third year middle school) music. The first song I taught was "Man-jiang-hong," a well-known song whose lyrics come from one of the classical poems by Yue Fei, a hero of the Song Dynasty. The title means: "The river is completely red." Some of my students tried to give me a hard time. "Teacher, sing it for us first." So I sang it and played the pedal-organ. After I finished, they were so impressed they stood up and applauded. After that, I felt much more comfortable.

Teaching in middle school, I felt more and more confident, especially in music class. For the school's tenth anniversary celebration, I selected a group of students, boys and girls, and we put together an opera. I produced it. I also composed all the music and wrote the lyrics. It was based on a classical historical story. It was an instant success. The local county magistrate and the head of the county education department attended the performance. Afterwards, they presented me with a certificate of merit.

Next, I wrote and produced another opera. It was an instant hit, too. It was the story of Qiu Jin, the female martyr who was executed in 1907 for leading an uprising to try to overthrow the Qing Dynasty.

My reputation grew. The provincial middle/high school in the Haizhou area noticed my talent and contacted me several times, trying to get me to change jobs. In 1928, I finally could not resist the higher pay and better reputation of that school, which was run by the province, not the county. I accepted the position with that school, teaching music and classical Chinese.

Many people were envious of the fact that I had landed such a good job. Some people said I got it because of connections, but the real reason was because I had that little bit of training and interest in music. Plus, I was fairly good at classical Chinese poetry. That's why I was able to get offered that attractive job.

At Haizhou, the first semester I taught eighth-grade Chinese. The best student in the class was a girl named Feng Xungu. She was highly capable and had a good understanding about the Chinese classics. So I always very seriously and carefully reviewed her assignments. One day she said, "My elder sister saw your comments on my composition, and she admires you very much. She would like to write a few essays and ask you to correct them."

I replied, "Of course."

Her elder sister, Feng Zixin, had begun attending nursing school in Zhenjiang, the provincial capital. But because she had been ill, Feng Zixin was recuperating at home. She loved writing and poetry and was eager to get someone to critique it.

A few days later, I saw Feng Zixin's essay and also a poem. Her writing was very mature and highly emotional. I carefully made my remarks and gave it back to her sister. After this, every week, I always had a chance to read some of her essays, and her younger sister was the messenger. For a long time, we never met each other.

One day Feng Zixin sent me a long poem. The title was "Seeing off the spring." It was not bad. The only thing was that toward the end, the words were not very tidy. So I made corrections. I wrote down four verses, like this: "When flowers bloom, they bloom quickly. When petals fall, they fall quickly. When beautiful things happen, they die quickly."

The next day, she sent me a letter, saying, "Teacher Yang: Your pen is very sharp. I have been wounded. Do you know that? Tonight why don't you come to my home with my sister and have dinner with us so that we can meet. Xin."

The first time I met her, I did not find that Feng Zixin was a beauty. But she had a pair of talking eyes and a very attractive mouth. In my life, she was like a pail of gasoline. All it would take was one lit match to burn both of us into ashes. I should never have lit the match.

From that point on, we often found reason to see one another. Often we met in the evenings at the city wall, just behind her family's back door. We held hands as we walked. Sometimes we just sat on the grass. Sometimes she talked endlessly; sometimes she sat very close to me without saying anything. Quickly, the match next to the pail of oil flashed and caught fire.

Feng Zixin was a very stubborn girl. She was like a silkworm, fabricating a cocoon around me. She tightened the threads and made me feel caught and confined, to the point where I became confused and frustrated. Still, I couldn't keep myself away from her.

She liked to lean against me in my arms. Often she would talk straight, nonstop, and then after finishing she would grab my hand and bite my fingers one by one. She would ask me, "Does it hurt?" When I said, "No," she got angry and said, "You don't even feel pain when I bite you. Maybe you don't even feel my love."

But if I said it hurt, she would also get angry, saying "If you feel pain when I bite you a little, how can we be willing to live together and die together in the future?" She talked in circles. It was hard to argue with her. She seemed to win every argument. Whenever I couldn't argue against her, I would tickle her until she gave up. Like a little mouse, she would snuggle tightly into my arms.

Happy days seemed to pass very quickly. Suddenly winter vacation arrived, and I had to go home to Nancheng. We knew we would have a sad separation. She saw me to the gate of the Haizhou city wall, and before departing she put a scarf that she knitted herself around my neck. She also stuck a letter in my pocket. Then she said: "Go. Don't turn back and look at me. Read the letter when you get home."

I walked away without looking back, and I didn't open the letter until I got home. When I opened it, there was only one sentence: "If you don't get divorced, I won't see you again."

In Nancheng, not only were there no people who had ever divorced, no one had ever even heard of it. I thought about it for several days. First, I tried to talk to my mother. The very word 'divorce' frightened her, and she just shook her head without saying a word. In the evening, I heard my father shouting at my mother, saying, "How could he want to send away someone like her? She never did anything wrong. We are not going to even discuss it." Clearly, my mother had talked to him. I felt the situation was ugly, so I quietly left the house.

I got a letter from Feng Zixin every day. Although she never mentioned divorce again in these letters, I felt very uneasy. Finally, I gathered enough courage to consult with my brother-in-law. He was a merchant and not a very articulate guy. After I told him what I had in mind, his face turned red. He was so angry he literally threw me out of his house. After that, I asked another relative to talk to my wife directly. She was a very gentle and honest person. After several discussions between them, she finally agreed, but with two conditions: One, she wanted to see her daughter, Huiling, all the time. Two, she asked me to give her a piece of land. So we divorced.

After the divorce, I wrote to Feng Zixin right away. She answered the letter immediately. I opened the letter. There was nothing written on the paper except the marks of her lips. By contrast, my father was really depressed. For several days, he refused to go out the door. He said he didn't have the courage to face other people.

After the New Year holiday, three days before school opened, I returned to school in Haizhou, primarily to see Feng Zixin. Aside from the times when we ate lunch or dinner, we spent every minute together, twisted like fabric. She jumped around like a little bird. The day before school started, we sat on the grass near the city wall. After sunset, a cold wind was blowing. She easily felt cold. In fact, that was the reason she had to temporarily stop her nursing school education. The doctor finally diagnosed a severe case of anemia. She was taking medicine for it every day.

When we were together, she always liked to take off her shoes and stick her feet under my long scholar's robe, all the way to touch my belly, both hands sticking into my long sleeves. I often took the end of my scarf, still partly wrapped around my neck, and wrapped it around her neck, too.

She asked me quietly, "When are you going to marry me?"

"Today," I said.

She shook her head.

"What do you want?" I asked.

She said, "After three years. I'd like to graduate from nursing school first."

Just at this time, a group of female students walked by, mostly classmates of her sister's, including her cousin, Feng Shujing. I was a little nervous and tried to get up on my feet. Feng Zixin said, "Don't move. If you're afraid about this, how can we get married?"

She turned around and told the girls: "We're playing hide and seek. He was caught by me. Would you like to come and join us?" The girls laughed and walked away.

Chapter Four

COMPLICATIONS

AFTER SCHOOL STARTED, the whole atmosphere seemed different. I felt everybody was looking at me with a different attitude. Feng Zixin's sister always kept a distance from me. But Feng Shujing, who was Feng Zixin's younger cousin, had the opposite reaction. She tried to get close to me. Sometimes, when she submitted her homework, she would add a slip of paper, asking me to meet her at a certain time and place. I always ignored that. One day she told me quietly, "Teacher Yang, the hide-and-seek story is known to everybody at school."

I continued to see Feng Zixin every evening, and we always met at the old place. We sometimes stayed together until deep in the night. She always wanted to walk me all the way back to my school, but I didn't feel safe letting her go back by herself, and therefore insisted on taking her back home. We went back and forth like this, past midnight. Every time we parted, we both felt a sense of sadness.

This life was like a painting. We were totally immersed in craziness and seemed to be drunk all the time. The days passed quickly.

After Chingming Festival in April 1929, the head of the junior high school asked me to meet him. At that time, students across the whole nation were involved in a movement to protest Japanese incursions into China. The principal asked me to produce an opera. The idea was to perform the show in the city to collect money for fighting against the Japanese army.

He patted me on the back and said, "Please do the best you can. I know you'll do very well. We heard that you just divorced and now you're seeing another woman and heavily involved in a love affair. You know, Haizhou is not Shanghai."

I said, "I know what I'm doing. Please don't worry."

In order to produce this particular opera, I had to do a lot of research and composition. To make time to do this, I had to ask the school to have a substitute teacher to take over some of my teaching assignments. Also, I had to ask Feng Zixin to meet me only twice a week. I immersed myself totally in this project. Still, no matter how busy I was, I thought about Feng Zixin. Often, after seeing her twice a week, I couldn't help but try to see her one more time.

She asked me, "What are you doing?"

I said, "I'm doing some overtime work." Then I would kiss her on her cheek and turn around and run away. When I came back to my work, I felt like I had more energy and became more productive.

In the middle of June, the show was performed three times in the nearby city of Xinpu. Afterwards, they added another show. The money collected was twice as much as originally expected. Everybody was very happy. The principal even gave me a gift as a reward. After the show, I got three days of vacation. Of course, I spent the whole three days with Feng Zixin.

One of those days we spent in a place called Shen Jia Yuan, about eight miles away from Xinpu. It was a beautiful garden, very quiet. Other than the birds singing, it was silent and serene. At noon, after eating lunch, I was tired. My head against her leg, I fell asleep. When I woke up, it was after sunset. We picked a lot of wild flowers, and she made a big flower ring out of it and put both of us together inside the ring. I said, "This feels like a wedding ceremony." She hit me pretty hard.

After the New Year holiday of 1930, Feng Zixin had to return to Zhenjiang to resume her nursing school. This made us both very sad.

"How often are you going to write me?" she asked me at the train station.

"Once a week," I said.

She shook her head.

"Every three days?"

She shook her head.

Then I said, "How about once a day?"

"No," she said. "I want three letters a day." Then she threw herself into my arms and started to cry. Then her father helped me to push her onto the train.

After she left, we wrote to each other often, at least every other day. Sometimes we wrote extremely long letters. But other times, when she was busy with her schoolwork, she would just send me a letter with one piece of paper, imprinted with her lips. When I was too busy to write, I would take a piece of paper and write three big characters: "Chang xiang si" – meaning, "Always thinking of you."

In the spring of 1930, the whole country started to boycott Japanese products. It was a movement that grew stronger every day. The school asked me to produce a few street dramas – plays to be shown on the streets in Haizhou City, in Xinpu, and in nearby towns and villages, as a way to spread the message to the public, to rouse the people's patriotic spirit. Primarily, I tried to take familiar folk tunes and substitute anti-Japanese lyrics, adding some dramatic acting performances.

One day, about two months after Feng Zixin left, I took a troupe to perform in the vicinity of Yang's Garden, and the title of the play was "Lay Down Your Whip." During the climax of the play, the main actress was being whipped, and the people watching the play were agitated. Some women were weeping and men were shouting. Suddenly, someone behind me tapped on my shoulder and said, "Cousin."

I turned my head and saw my cousin Wu Xiulian. I was in shock. She quickly introduced me to her husband, who was standing beside her. He was a very big man, somewhat fat and rough. Very awkwardly, I asked her, "How are you, cousin?"

She bowed her head and replied in a quiet voice, "Hao shemma" – meaning, 'What's so good about it?' – adding, "It was better when I was young."

I felt a little dizzy. Quickly the show ended, and I said goodbye to both of them. I went back to school. On the way back, I was talking to myself, repeating what she said, "It was better when I was young."

Right behind me was Feng Shujing. She had been the main actress in the play, playing the part of the woman who was being whipped. She could sing very well and she was attractive, so she had been selected to play the main character. She asked me, "Teacher, is it true that you haven't received a letter from your mother for a long time?" I did not reply. I just walked straight to the faculty housing where I lived.

That night I was very tired, but I couldn't go to sleep. My short glimpse of my cousin, Wu Xiulian, brought back all the memories of my childhood love for her. I got out of bed, opened the window, and looked out at the bright moonlight and stars, noticing how the trees in the darkness shook in the cold wind. Suddenly it reminded me of Feng Zixin. She was always afraid of the cold. Now she was all by herself, living alone in a faraway place. I couldn't even keep her hands and feet warm. I returned to my desk and wrote a very long letter to her.

After I finished, it was daybreak. My head felt heavy and hot. I was sick.

About noon, a young man who was my elder cousin came with the school physician, who gave me a shot and left some medicine. That cousin asked one of the laborers at the school to take care of me. He asked that no student should disturb me. During my illness, I missed my mother very much and also Feng Zixin. I thought if my mother could put her hand on my forehead, my headache would be gone. If Feng Zixin could put her feet on my belly, then I probably would be able to eat something.

Deep in the night, when I was in a state of half-dreaming, half-conscious, I felt a hand touching my head. When I opened my eyes, I saw that it was Feng Shujing, who stood by my bed. I asked her what time it was. She said, "It's not ten yet." I said, "You'd better go away. At 10:00 the door of the school will be closed. Please don't come again."

After she left, I started to think: this girl is a little bit abnormal. She seemed precocious for a fifteen-year-old. Her writing was not particularly good, yet she always wrote in the contemporary style, which at the time was beginning to be very popular. Maybe, I thought, I should teach her a little more so that she would not go in the wrong direction.

My illness lasted three days. After recovering, I began to be busy again. But what made me happiest was receiving two letters from Feng Zixin and also a wool vest, knitted by her personally. She hadn't realized I was sick, and she complained that I didn't write enough. She said, "I don't want you to write 'Thinking of you always.' I only want long letters." She said she had knitted the vest at night. "I was thinking of you when I was knitting the vest for you. Sometimes I cried when I was doing that. So all my tears and my love went into this vest."

I also received some get-well letters from other students: some from high-school students, some from junior high students, some from boys, some from girls. There were two letters from Feng Shujing. I wasn't impressed by her letters.

One day, during a very heavy rain, I received a letter from my father, delivered to me by someone he sent. The letter said my sister, Da-mei, was extremely sick. He asked me to come home as soon as possible, to see her for the last time.

My sister had been married for two years. She did not get along with her husband. They had a baby son called Jiang Daquan. She was so unhappy in her marriage that she had talked about committing suicide. After seeing the letter, I rushed home. What I found out was this: She had had a big argument with her brother-in-law, known as Wang-Yeh, "Little Emperor." She suffered a lot of abuse, and he had hit her. After the beating, she stole a piece of opium from her father-in-law and swallowed it.

When I saw her, she was near death. I cried loudly and called her name. She responded by nodding her head. Shortly after that, she died.

I was devastated. I ran out to look for this Little Emperor, and I didn't find him, but I found my brother-in-law, her husband. I grabbed him and beat him up. His parents kneeled on the ground and asked me to forgive their family. I came home, crying all the way. My mother was hysterical, and my father was quietly weeping beside her. My second younger sister, Er-mei, was holding Daquan, the baby, only six months old. She was feeding him rice soup. From that day, Daquan lived in our house, with our family. My parents refused to give him back to the Jiang family.

Da-mei was only one year younger than I was. When we were little, we were very close. Secrets I wouldn't tell anyone else, I would confide in her. When she got married, I paid for the expenses, including all her dowry. When Huiling was a little girl, Damei made all her shoes, clothes, skirts, and even the bows for her hair.

That night, I did not sleep at all. I finally wrote a letter to Feng Zixin. I heard the little baby crying in the next room. I pitied that poor little boy.

Da-mei was the eldest of eight sisters I had, and all of them died young. My second sister, Er-mei, lived to be a teenager but died before she was old enough to marry. After those eight daughters, my mother had one last child, another son, whom they called Yang Jinnan. He was almost the same age as my daughter, Huiling, and they grew up together. He is the only one of my siblings who grew to adulthood and led a normal life.

After I returned to school, there was a long letter from Feng Zixin waiting for me. It covered ten pages. She was worried about my sickness. She said, "I wish I could be there with you, in your arms. Then maybe you wouldn't have gotten sick."

When I was concentrating and reading the letter, Feng Shujing walked into my room quietly. She said, "I've been here for a while."

I didn't answer.

"Is that a letter from your mother?" she asked.

"Why do you have to know?" I countered.

She walked away, unhappily.

Chapter Five

STREET DRAMA

I STARTED PUTTING all my effort into my work and wrote several new plays and organized two more troupes. The actors and singers were all students from the high school. I took them to a lot of places to perform. I tried to avoid working with Feng Shujing. But she seemed to always find a way to come to my side. She often came to my room, asking questions.

In a letter, I asked Feng Zixin, "Why is she always hanging around here when she knows I really don't want to see her?"

She replied, "If you're talking about Feng Shujing, please don't worry. Also, don't make her too embarrassed by obviously rejecting her. She is basically a child."

Later on, I found out that Feng Zixin's own sister had written to her, also warning her that Feng Shujing was acting rather abnormally toward me.

That summer vacation, Feng Zixin originally was planning to be back at home. We were going to do some sightseeing. But her nursing school moved from Zhenjiang to Nanjing, and she was assigned to a work/study program. Therefore, she couldn't break away to come home. At the same time, my school was notified by the provincial education department that they had organized all the music teachers of the whole province, about 70 people, to come to Haizhou Middle/High School to learn and study the street drama and opera that I had composed. So I was very excited. Obviously, I had attracted positive attention from the provincial government. Feng Zixin was also very encouraging of my work.

During summer vacation, the principal of my school gave me 200 yuan as a production fee. He said, "It seems you have done enough street dramas. I'd like to have you start to compose a long musical, which we can produce as a play, as long as eight to ten hours. The play can be shown on three consecutive days." This sounded challenging to me, and I felt awkward about it. But I had to promise to do it. In order to compose the musical, I put in all my time and effort. The title of the play was "White-Haired Concubine." The story came from a Tang poem, which goes:

The ancient palace is lonely.
The flowers in the palace shine red in the sun.
The palace concubines' hair turns white.
They sit and gossip about the emperor.

That poem reflects the sadness and loneliness of women in the palace, where they wasted their youth and their beauty and seldom even saw the emperor.

The play I composed was based on an aging palace concubine, reliving her memories. It took place during the late history of the Tang Dynasty. That was the same time as the famous love affair between Emperor Tang Minghuang and the beautiful Yang Guifei, who were so much in love that the emperor ignored affairs of state.

My plan was to write a play with nine acts, to be performed over three days. Each act would be about one hour. So each day's performance would be three hours. I wrote to Feng Zixin and told her all about it. She was very enthusiastic and supportive.

After I finished writing the play, again Feng Shujing tried to get one of the main roles. I had to make some excuse, saying that these decisions would have to be made by somebody else. Finally, she got a very small part in the play, and she wasn't very happy.

The actual play was not performed until January of 1931. Originally this was going to be performed just for the provincial music school teachers and students. It turned out that many more people came to see it. During the day of the show, the whole auditorium was filled with people. At the last minute, they had to remove all the younger students from the audience to make room for all the adults who wanted to see it.

It was a huge success. The provincial education department gave me an award of two silver cups. February 3 was Feng Zixin's birthday. I sent both silver cups to her as my birthday present. She wrote back, saying, "You gave me such a wonderful and heavy gift! I hope we can use these cups after we are married, to celebrate during our wedding night."

Chapter Six

SUBTLE THREATS

BOTH OF US NUMBERED OUR LETTERS to each other. During the winter holiday, I spent some time putting her letters together, in order. I discovered that two letters were missing. I couldn't find them anywhere.

Then, just before Chinese New Year, I got a letter from Feng Shujing. She asked me: "Can I come to visit you and your family in Nancheng for a couple of days?"

I replied by letter, saying "No."

But during the second day of Chinese New Year, she and her sister, who was in 7th grade, showed up at my home. I felt extremely awkward. My mother liked both of them. Huiling and my younger brother, Jinnan, also liked them. Jinnan and Huiling were about six or seven. The girls played with the little ones. On the third day of their visit, they left.

I wrote a letter to Feng Zixin and told her about the whole thing. She wrote back, saying, "I don't see anything wrong if a student comes to visit her teacher. You shouldn't be so sensitive about it."

After school opened again, I went to see a distant aunt (guma) to give her new year wishes. Her husband didn't stay at home often because he had a concubine somewhere else. So at home were only my aunt and her 15-year-old daughter, plus an amah. They had a very large house in Haizhou and leased out several rooms to students. My aunt told me she had just leased a room to two sisters named Feng. "They said they are both your students. They told me they spent Chinese New Year at your house, and they like your daughter very much."

After hearing that, I began to understand. Feng Shujing's hometown was 50 Chinese li away from the school. During the school year, she and her sister had to live in the city by renting a room at a house. It was such a coincidence that she would rent a room from my aunt. After a little while, Feng Shujing showed up. We talked a little bit, and she invited me to see her room. It had two beds and one desk. It looked very clean and comfortable. After a while, I left and went back to school.

During that spring, I felt a little lazy. One Sunday, I did not go home. In the afternoon, I slept. Suddenly, Feng Shujing was knocking at my door. She said my aunt was sick and asked me to visit her. I ran over, and her daughter said she had recovered after taking some medicine and was now sleeping. So Feng Shujing asked me to go to her room to sit. I felt it would be awkward to say no, so I went in. Then I realized that her younger sister had gone home. So we were alone.

After I sat down, she took out her Chinese literature textbook and started to ask me different kinds of questions. She also picked up a copy of "Dream of the Red Chamber" and asked many rather sensitive questions. I did not answer most of them. I found an excuse and left.

When Feng Shujing turned in her assignment book to me, she always put a little note in it. At one point, she wrote, "Why did you get a divorce? For whom?" I felt somewhat annoyed. So I asked the school authorities to switch me to a different class. They refused.

Once, my aunt asked me to come over for dinner. After dinner, she smoked a water-pipe and we talked. She said the Yang family's ancestors did not accumulate enough good deeds; that explained our misfortune. "After your grandfather died, there were no more *xiucai* in the family," she said. *Xiucai* is the title for a man who has passed the initial ranking of the imperial exam. She told me her husband had a concubine, who lived elsewhere, which made her life very sad.

"And now, I hear you just divorced your wife. This is all very regrettable for our family," she said. "Recently, I also heard that you started having a love affair with someone. You'd better control yourself and not further damage the family's reputation. How many girls have you seen who are having so-called open love affairs who are good girls? Most of them wind up being concubines."

I sensed that all this information was planted by Feng Shujing. I decided I'd better not even talk to Feng

Shujing anymore. She had gone too far, trying to damage my reputation in front of my aunt.

Before summer vacation in 1931, I went through the letters I had received from Feng Zixin. I discovered that three more were missing, according to the numbers written on each one. I wondered.

After I went home, I organized all the operas and dramas I had written, and I felt a deep sense of pride. I invited an old school buddy, Lu Deju, who had studied kunqu opera with me, to come to stay with me for a few days and read my work. After he got through reading my works, he raised two suggestions, which I accepted.

Lu Deju was a very smart man, very emotional and sensitive, and also very righteous. The only problem with him was that he wasn't very motivated in terms of improving himself. Therefore he always had difficulty keeping his job. In fact, I recommended him twice for teaching positions in elementary schools. In both cases, he didn't stay very long. Therefore, he seemed to be poor all the time, always complaining. Every time I saw him, I gave him some money. He always accepted, with a blush on his face.

One day, I received a letter from Feng Shujing. She suggested that I should accompany her to visit Lianyungang. Also in the letter, there were some sarcastic comments, such as, "I'm just a poor little girl. Nobody wants to warm my hands and my feet and cuddle me." Because of this and other comments of hers, I concluded that all five missing letters from Feng Zixin must have been stolen by Feng Shujing. I found myself in a very awkward situation.

With some reluctance, I told Lu Deju everything about the two Feng girls. Because Lu Deju was my closest friend, I hoped he could give me some advice. He first asked me whether or not I planned to go to Lianyungang with Feng Shujing.

"No way. I'm not going to go," I said.

Then he shook his head and said, "You must understand. There are some subtle threats in this letter. What she is implying is that she knows what's going on between you and her cousin, Feng Zixin, and all your secrets. She has proof in the form of those letters. If she's really desperate, if she discloses all these letters to her family and to the school where you're teaching, maybe even some of the local newspapers, then you must think: under our current feudalistic society, can you sustain such damage? What about Feng Zixin? Can she sustain this kind of scandal? Both your families will also suffer from this kind of disclosure."

This thought had not occurred to me. But I could see that he was right. It would be extremely damaging to my reputation if news of my love affair got out. "What do you think I should do?" I asked.

"You must be patient, trying to play along with her," he advised. "But secretly ask Feng Zixin to marry you sooner. As soon as you get married, then Feng Shujing will no longer have leverage over you."

I took in all his suggestions, and it appeared to me that I had no other options. But, of course, if I took Shujing alone for a tour of Lianyungang, it could also cause a scandal. So we finally decided that Lu Deju and I would go together, inviting along another old high school classmate, a girl. So we made such plans, and then at the same time I wrote a long letter to Feng Zixin and asked her to agree to marry me in the winter of 1931. Originally we were planning to be married in the summer of 1933, after she graduated from nursing school.

Three of us arrived in Lianyungang according to plan. Feng Shujing had arrived earlier. We all stayed in the home of one of my distant cousins, Mr. Yang Naizhuang. He had a very large house, a big courtyard and a garden. At that time, both he and his wife were also teaching at a local elementary school.

That same afternoon we went to the beach. We watched the ocean, the seagulls flying, the sun setting like a huge fireball falling behind the distant mountains. I had taken a flute with me and I played it. At that time, I was very good at it. At the time, all I could think of was how nice it would be if Feng Zixin could be there with me, alone, in my arms. I knew she would love to listen to my flute music. After dark, when Lu Deju and the other girl were walking ahead of us, Feng Shujing suddenly turned to me and asked, very seriously, "Are you going to marry my cousin, Feng Zixin?"

I didn't want anyone talking about Feng Zixin behind her back, so I avoided answering the question. Instead I said, "My mother asked me to marry a cousin of mine. My father basically agreed. Both of them prefer me not to marry a female student."

"Did you agree?" she asked.

I hesitated. "I'm trying to drag it out. Eventually, I may have to agree."

After that, she seemed more relaxed. She laughed and grabbed my hand, and she asked me, in a very low voice, "What would happen if your aunt tried to match us up?"

I said, "Aren't you a female student?"

Actually, what I told her was not entirely false. My mother had the idea of asking me to marry her sister's daughter. She had a round face and was a little fat, not very attractive. She didn't know how to read. My mother knew I would not be willing to accept that. Therefore, she did not mention it again.

Chapter Seven

EMBARRASSING EXPERIENCES

SOON AFTER THAT, my aunt went back to Nancheng to visit her relatives. I was a little concerned, so I told my mother about the possibility that she may bring up the idea of my marrying Feng Shujing.

My mother said, "No, that's not right. She's too young. What you need is someone who is at least twenty."

I said, "Don't worry about that. Just don't offend her. Just say we'll talk about it later."

My mother had met Feng Shujing only once. So when my aunt came to Nancheng and brought it up, my mother agreed to say, "I don't think that's possible. She's only a few years older than his daughter, Huiling. If he wants to marry again, he should marry someone at least twenty years old."

A couple days later, my aunt did show up. She started saying, "Look, you need a good daughter-in-law in this household. I know someone." She started talking about Feng Shujing.

My mother said, "It's very nice of you to bring this up. I must talk to my son about this. Maybe you can let me have her birthday and horoscope, so I can check it out." That was the custom of the time, to compare the precise time of birth for two prospective marriage partners and ask a fortune-teller to predict what kind of future they might have together.

Ten days later, Feng Shujing sent me a long, corny letter. Also, she mentioned her time of birth and horoscope. Basically, she asked me to make an early decision. I wrote and told Feng Zixin all about this.

Feng Zixin wrote back with a lot of excitement. She said that her parents had basically agreed we could get married during the winter holiday of 1931. I did not tell this to my mother. At the same time, I tried to keep Feng Shujing at bay. It was a very long, hot summer vacation.

When school started, Feng Zixin sent her letters to me through her sister. This way would be safer. One day, Feng Shujing asked me to meet her at her aunt's house. She also invited her sister and another aunt's husband. At that time, this man was the Kuomintang Party secretary for all of Haizhou County. I felt there was some formality in this whole discussion. My aunt asked me about my birthday and horoscope. I said, "My mother has looked over the birthday and horoscope, and she's being very careful, as an old lady. There might be some problem according to one expert we consulted. Now she's getting a second opinion."

Then, the aunt's husband started to say that now we all live in the new age, and for a young man and woman to get married, the most important thing is to have love. Horoscope and birthday should not be considered as deciding factors.

Feng Shujing said, "Well, I already met his mother, Auntie Yang. She's very kind and nice. I'm sure she would not object."

After her aunt's husband left, Feng Shujing suddenly became very serious and asked, "Now today, we have talked over everything in front of my aunt. You must make a decision that you are going to marry me."

Her aunt was laughing, and I said, "To marry a girl is not like buying eggs. You must be careful." Everybody laughed.

Feng Shujing was standing right next to me. She pinched my thigh. Then I found some excuse and left. Feng Shujing walked me to the front door. As soon as we got outside the door, she jumped up and kissed me on the cheek.

Just during this very awkward time, where I had to report all these embarrassing experiences to Feng Zixin and also to play along with Feng Shujing, the 9-1-8 incident took place. This was the invasion of northeastern China by Japan on September 18, 1931. By coincidence, that was my 24th birthday. The whole country was in turmoil, particularly the students. Everybody was screaming, "Kill the Japanese bandits." My students in Haizhou joined in the protests.

The principal of my school was also very politically active. He often took a group of students to the streets and gave a speech. I had to take a group of students to perform on the streets. With all this going on, we were very disappointed that some of the local merchants still sold Japanese products.

During this time of turmoil, Feng Zixin's younger sister came to me one day and told me that Feng Zixin was very sick with a bad case of malaria. "She is getting severe chills and has to cover herself with three quilts. She asked me not to tell you, so you wouldn't be worried," the sister said.

I was so worried after hearing this that I decided to go to Nanjing to see her. But I could not. First, the school refused to let me go. Second, the railroad at that time was very unsafe. After Xuzhou, sometimes the Japanese would destroy the tracks and cause trouble. Plus, I kept getting letters from Feng Zixin saying that I should not come to Nanjing. At this point, she looked so bad she didn't want me to see her. She told me she was getting much better. She said, "By winter vacation, I will be all well, with my original pretty face." Therefore, I decided not to go. But I borrowed about 100 yuan from the school and sent it to her.

Feng Zixin's parents asked me to see them and talk about the arrangements for the wedding in the coming winter vacation. I agreed with all their arrangements. They said, "These are all Feng Zixin's ideas. She's very meticulous." Afterwards, they asked me if I had started looking for a job in Nanjing. I told them that my distant uncle was working as chief engineer in the Ministry of Hydraulics.

"He will be looking out for jobs for me. I don't think it will be a problem," I said. "After we get married, I'm not going to let Feng Zixin live in Nanjing by herself."

The weather was getting colder, but I felt warm in my heart, day by day. Every day was getting closer to my pending marriage. At last I would be able to marry the woman I loved, Feng Zixin.

Chapter Eight

MAJOR MANIPULATION

ONE WEEKEND, I returned home to my parents' house and spent time trying to clean up the house. Suddenly something happened. Feng Shujing's younger sister came rushing to me and said, "My sister just attempted to commit suicide. She cut her wrists, and she's bleeding."

I went with her and rushed to her house. I saw Feng Zixin's younger sister, holding Feng Shujing's arm and putting bandages on her. There was a knife on the floor, not too much blood, but Feng Shujing was crying and screaming. She said I was a cheater. "What's the point of staying alive?"

Then Feng Zixin's sister explained. "Feng Shujing came to our house to have lunch with us. She saw that my mother had bought some new silk fabric. Feng Shujing asked, 'Is that going to be used for the bride?' My mother just smiled. Feng Shujing decided it must mean that you and my sister are going to get married. She started to cry, and I took her home. Then she started to cut her wrists.

We were all so scared. She wouldn't listen to anybody. I'm going to go now."

Before she left, she turned around and said, "Actually, that fabric was purchased by my cousin. She's going to get married in the winter."

At that time, Feng Shujing seemed to have calmed down. She said, "I read the letters that Feng Zixin sent to you. I can see that she wants to marry you and she always wanted to marry you. From those letters, I can see that you have a very deep love and commitment. But I loved you much earlier. You should know that. But you always try to avoid me. I'm very jealous. I can't stand that. I'm younger than she is. I don't think she's much better looking than I am. Why do you love her instead? Today, let me tell you clearly: If you don't want to marry me, I might as well die. I'm going to disclose all the letters to Feng Zixin's family. I'm going to tell the school and the newspapers. Maybe all three of us will die together."

She was talking such crazy talk that it seemed likely she really would kill herself and try to destroy me, too. In today's world, it may be hard to imagine, but in those days, public proof of a love affair prior to marriage would bring a scandal that could ruin a girl's reputation for life and cause a man to be fired from his job in shame. I had to say something, anything, to calm her down. So I lied.

"First, Feng Zixin and I are just friends," I insisted. "Second, that fabric was for her cousin, who is getting married. Third, if we want to get married, both sets of parents have to agree. My parents might be easy to convince. What about your parents?"

I knew that her family was a typical feudalistic family. Her father was very domineering and rich. They even had guard towers on their house, with armed body guards. I didn't believe he would let his daughter marry a poor teacher, divorced, eight years older than she was.

Then she said, "I don't care. I have decided I'm going to marry you, for sure. I'm going to ask my uncle to talk to my parents. They're going to agree. But you must assure me today. We must go to take a picture together. Go with me now."

What else could I say at this point? So we went to a photo studio and got our picture taken together. Afterwards, I took her to a small restaurant. She became very happy and excited again. She said, "We had our picture taken together and we went out for dinner. This is the date of our engagement."

I felt extremely awkward and sad beyond measure. How could I, a 24-year-old acclaimed teacher, have let myself be manipulated and trapped by a high school girl? It seemed impossible. And yet it had happened.

On our way back, I was afraid we might bump into somebody who knew us. So we walked with some distance between us. As we passed by the back door of Feng Zixin's house, it was late autumn and a cold wind was blowing. In the evening light, everything I saw there reminded me of Feng Zixin. It seemed that she was asking me, with tears in her eyes, "What are you doing?"

When I got back to my dorm room, it was after ten p.m. I started writing to Feng Zixin immediately. Before I knew it, my letter was ten pages long. After daybreak, I took the letter to a mailbox and came back to sleep, exhausted. When I woke up, it was already past noon. After I got up, I went to a little restaurant and ate some dumplings. Then I walked by myself to a nearby garden. In the bright autumn afternoon, leaves were falling and birds were flying across the sky. The whole world seemed impossibly sad. I felt I had lost control of my life and didn't know what to do. I found myself crying.

On my way back, I decided to pick up the picture we had taken the previous day. When I arrived, the shopkeeper told me that the girl had already picked up the picture. When I got back to my room, there was a letter from Feng Shujing on my desk. I opened it. Inside, there was a copy of the picture. It said, "Engagement Day."

Chapter Nine

THE STORM BREAKS

ON MONDAY MORNING, after morning exercises, Feng Zixin's sister came by and gave me a letter from Feng Zixin. She wrote that she had fully recovered from malaria. "Don't worry." She said she had received the money I sent her and would use it to buy a lot of nutritious food so she could recover more quickly. "You may regret this! By the time you marry me during winter vacation, your bride may be as big as a water barrel," she wrote. "Honestly, I feel each day is longer than a year."

Although it was a short letter, I enjoyed it so much. Her happiness and sweetness jumped off the page. I thought, soon she will receive the long letter I wrote yesterday. She will complain about her mother letting out the secret. Maybe she would be so worried she would come back to see me right away.

That evening, I sent a letter to Lu Deju, asking him to come back to visit me. He was a few years older than I, and sometimes his mind was clearer than mine. In a situation like this, I believed he could help me.

Everything pointed to a storm coming my way. I felt extremely uneasy. My mind seemed to draw a blank. Sometimes I felt like a pole was striking my head. Then, I would get a mental image of Feng Zixin and hear her words. She felt so far away.

One day, a man came to ask me to go to the office of the county Party secretary, who was Feng Shujing's aunt's husband. So I went. He was very polite. He said, "Mr. Yang, I like you. I know you are quite scholarly in our county. Also I know that Feng Shujing loves you very much. Although she's quite a bit younger than you are, I don't think that's a major problem. I'd like to see your divorce paper. If everything is in order, I could talk to her parents. I think we can get this thing settled."

I happened to have the divorce paper in my wallet. I took it out and showed it to him. He looked at me and nodded. He was satisfied, so he let me leave.

When I got home, Lu Deju was sleeping on my bed. I went to teach two music classes. When I came back, he was still sleeping, so I woke him up. It was evening. We went to a little dumpling restaurant and then I took him to a friend's house where he could stay. After that, we went to a little teahouse and talked. I told him about the latest developments with the two Feng girls. He was puffing cigarettes, one after another. After I finished talking, the teahouse was about to close.

All he could say was: "Big trouble."

We decided to come back the following evening, same time, same place, to continue our conversation. The second day, when we met, the first thing he said was, "You're really stupid. How can you not know that in our society, to have a love affair is worse than taking a concubine? How you got yourself into such deep trouble, I really don't understand. I thought about it last night. The problem is this: Feng Zixin loves you with fierce intensity. And Feng Shujing is determined to get you and even die for you. Now it looks like you're not going to be able to avoid calamity. The question is: How can you minimize the damage?"

I asked him when he was planning to go back. He said, "It's not important when I go back. Anyway, I don't have a fixed job. Your problem could escalate into a crisis at any moment. I cannot just leave you here and go home. I regret I ever made a friend like you."

Finally, I stuck some more money in his pocket. I said, "I'll see you again tomorrow. Same time, same place."

A week passed. I saw Feng Shujing only once during that week. She told me that during the New Year, January 1, her uncle was planning to visit her parents. As for Feng Zixin, after that short letter, I never received another letter. I wondered if she was sick again.

One day, after my morning class, I returned to my room. Feng Zixin's sister came to my place, crying. She said, "One of my sister's letters to you was stolen again. I put the letter in my coat pocket, and after the morning class, when I came back, it wasn't there." I said, "Go back." I thought: "Boy, I may have a big problem again." I was hoping this letter was not stolen by Feng Shujing.

The next class I was going to teach was the Chinese literature class where Feng Shujing was one of the students. When I walked into the classroom, I discovered she wasn't there. I thought: "Calamity has arrived."

My mind was in total confusion. I could not think straight at all. When I finished that class, I had to teach two other classes, in music. After that, I returned to my room and lay down on my bed, sweating.

Then Feng Shujing's sister came. She said that her sister asked me to meet her at noon.

So I went. I felt like a criminal going to court when I walked into Feng Shujing's room. She was crying so hard. Her eyes were red and puffy. Tears covered her face. With shaking hands, I picked up the letter, which was in Feng Zixin's familiar handwriting. Here's what it said:

My dear,

I received your long letter and every word poked straight into my heart and caused it to bleed. I cried for the whole night. I don't understand why Heaven would punish us so mercilessly. After long consideration, I made the following decisions.

1. You asked me to marry you during the winter holidays. Of course, I agreed, but now things have changed. If we wait until winter holiday, it may be too late. Anything could happen during this time. I cannot come home and have the wedding there, because I know that Feng Shujing's father can be very unreasonable. He

loves Shujing very much. He could even kill people for her. Also, her uncle is a very powerful man in the county. If Shujing is willing to die over this, we all could die together if I come back.

2. Here's the new plan. We must get married in Nanjing on January 1st. You had better come quietly, a few days before. My father would come for the wedding. But you'd better not come in the same bus. Your parents probably shouldn't come, since you have an uncle in Nanjing.

3. I already found an apartment. I am going to prepare everything. You could find a job. Even if you can't, I have enough money. I earn 50 yuan every month, working part time in the hospital. It would be enough for both of us.

4. Before you come to Nanjing, it's better if you don't go back to Nancheng. If anybody discovers our plan, you may not be able to come. Try to act normally in school and especially in front of Shujing. You don't even have to take anything from your room or go visit my parents.

5. We have less than 30 days before January 1. As long as you can walk out of that train station in Nanjing, I'm going to grab you and keep you for the rest of my life.

One thousand kisses.

Feng Zixin had signed it with a lot of red kiss marks.

After I read the letter, I understood how serious this was. I felt like I was in the eye of the storm. Feng Shujing looked at me like an angry wolf. She grabbed the letter from my trembling hand, then asked me: "What is your explanation to me?"

I stuttered, "What do you want me to do?"

She said, "I want you to elope with me. Will you agree?"

Shocked, I stared at her. Then I nodded my head. At the time, I didn't think I could give her any other answer.

Then she said, "Good. Now listen carefully. First, today and tomorrow, you make all the plans for the elopement. On the morning of the third day, at six o'clock, I will be in front of the church near the West Gate of the city. If you see me holding a letter in my hand and putting that letter into the mailbox in front of the church, that means I am mailing a letter to my parents to say goodbye. You must walk toward me and we will go together from there. Second, if after 6:10, you don't show in front of the church, I will come back and kill myself immediately."

Then she picked up a little case and took out a knife and a bottle of pills and also a bunch of letters. "After I die, everybody will know that I was cheated by you. You must be prepared to go to jail. Third, if by chance I change my mind during the coming two days, I will show up at the church that morning, but I will not drop a letter into the mailbox. Then I will tell you what I'll do after that."

Chapter Ten

INTO A BOTTOMLESS WELL

I QUICKLY RETURNED to the school and taught my next two classes. After that, I ran to Lu Deju's place. He hadn't woken up yet. I told him about all the latest developments. He was scratching his head, looking amazed and very sad.

After a while, he said, "There's a chance she will change her mind. Maybe she will realize that you will never really love her – and that it's a terrible thing to kill herself. Otherwise, I'm afraid you don't have much choice. You'd better prepare some money in the next few days. I'll try to find two reliable rickshaws. Then we'll see each other on the morning of the third day in front of the church." Then he shook his head, adding with a grim smile, "Maybe it's a good idea she chose to meet you in front of a church. Maybe God will make her change her mind."

I returned to school, still in shock but trying to look and act normally. I went to the accounting office to borrow some money. I also wrote to Feng Zixin and told her what had happened. Then I wrote to my uncle in Nanjing, asking him to look for a job for me. One way or another, my life was about to change drastically. It all seemed unreal.

Those two days felt like twenty years.

On the morning of the third day, at 5:30, Lu Deju and I got to the church at the same time. There were two rickshaws sitting there, with two pullers, and Lu Deju's bicycle was leaning against a wall. Both pullers were young and strong. It was very cold and the wind was blowing. My heart was beating faster and faster.

At 5:55, I saw Feng Shujing coming. I was hoping she would go straight into the church instead of to the mailbox. But she went to the mailbox directly. She hesitated for a moment, and then she dropped the letter.

My mind went blank. I felt like I had just fallen into a bottomless well. We didn't speak to each other. Quietly, we each got in a rickshaw and took off.

Lu Deju rode his bicycle beside us, in front of us, and behind us. He was very alert, like a general running up and down the battlefield. I turned back and looked at Phoenix Mountain, which overlooks Nancheng. I thought about my family, about my parents. How could they make a living without my support? My mother's health was not very good at the time. How would she sustain this tremendous blow? My father was always concerned about his reputation. He would suffer a lot from the cruel gossip of people in the community.

As I was thinking about all this, we arrived in the next town, called Banpu. When we went through the streets, both Feng Shujing and I pulled up our scarves and covered our faces up to our eyes. Lu Deju was wearing sunglasses. Nothing went wrong. After we passed through the South Gate, Lu Deju bought a bunch of steamed bread and meat buns and gave some to each of us to eat as we rode along.

After dark, we reached another little town called Yangjiaji. At that point, we had already traveled 130 Chinese li, or 43 miles. That was our first planned stop.

After dinner, Feng Shujing and I slept in a back room of a small inn. Lu Deju slept on a big table outside the room. After some struggle, I gave in. That was the first time I committed sin with Feng Shujing. To her, if I didn't do it, she would never trust me. As for me, I was not willing and I felt terribly guilty. I asked myself: How am I ever going to face Feng Zixin?

When the rooster started to sing, around four o'clock in the morning, Lu Deju asked us to get up. He said, "Ten li down the road is a river. After six, the tide will recede, and it will be very difficult to cross."

We rushed to get to the river while it was still high tide. We quickly got on a boat and crossed the river. Then we found a place to have breakfast. We ate some steamed bread and rice porridge. It tasted really good. Feng Shujing changed her attitude completely. She became very lively and talkative. Sometimes, she would tear off a piece of bread and stuff it into my mouth.

But I felt very sad, looking at the sky, looking at the trees, looking at the dishes of food. In everything I saw the image of Feng Zixin.

Chapter Eleven

CHASED BY ARMED GUARDS

I LOOKED AT MY WATCH, which had been given to me by my old friend, Qiu Menglin. It was 6:30 a.m. Lu Deju said: "Let's get on the road again."

Then from across the river, we suddenly heard the sound of gunshots. We could see the dust from the bullets hitting the river bank near us.

Feng Shujing was very scared. She said, "It must be the armed guards from my family, chasing after us."

Lu Deju said, "Don't worry. If they want to cross the river, they'll have to wait till 5 p.m. By that time, we'll be long gone. Let's get going."

The river was swathed in fog. We could not see the faces of the people on the other side. Of course, they couldn't see us, either. So we got on the rickshaws and urged our pullers to run quickly.

After ten o'clock, we reached the town of Funing. Then we sent the rickshaws off. We gave the pullers a little more money and told them not to say anything about us to anybody.

After buying some food, we walked to another river and hired a small boat. We told the boat driver to take us to Xinghua. There were a lot of river routes in that area. Xinghua was a little out of the way, so we felt that was a safe place to be.

That boat was very nice. It had a table and chairs on the deck. They served us tea. By that time, Feng Shujing and Lu Deju seemed to know each other very well, like old friends. They started to talk and play cards. They relaxed, but I still felt tense.

After 24 hours on this boat, the next morning we arrived in Xinghua. We found a small inn and settled down. In those days, no one had identity cards. Feng Shujing put her name on the register as Ma Zhen. I put my name as Li Yuan. Lu Deju posed as my younger brother, Li Da. According to the hotel's rule, we took rooms for three people, including food. The charge was 30 yuan a month. I immediately gave the innkeeper 30 yuan for the first month.

We felt we had made it to safety.

After a couple of days, boredom set in. Lu Deju went to the store and bought an erhu, a two-stringed violin, and a xiao, a Chinese flute. He was very good at playing the erhu, and I was very good at playing the flute. We started playing these instruments. Sometimes the guests in the other rooms came to listen to us.

But after a while, Feng Shujing became restless. She did not even like to have us play these instruments. Sometimes I felt so bored, I went next door to talk to Lu

Deju. Then after an hour, Feng Shujing would throw all the teacups and teapots and even the lamps on the floor. I really felt very awkward and embarrassed. My heart felt very pained and sad, but I had to try to comfort her. Sometimes in the middle of the night, I would weep. It felt like I had reached the end of the earth. It seemed to me that whenever hardships hit in life, they always hit hard, like a big storm.

One night, Feng Shujing suddenly said she had a terrible headache. Afterwards, she wanted to drink a lot of water. She was so hot she felt like a fireball. I didn't know what to do. Lu Deju asked the manager at the front desk, who was a kind, elderly man.

He looked at her and shook his head. "This is terrible," he said. "You must get a doctor right away. I know one of the local doctors here. He charges 10 yuan for a visit, in advance." Lu Deju took the money and went to the clinic to get Dr. Fang.

After the doctor came and examined her, he decided that she had typhoid fever. "It's lucky you didn't delay," he said. "She needs to take five doses of medicine, which I have here. She should be okay." Strangely enough, after she took these five doses of medicine, she was fine. But we spent 30 yuan for all of that.

Finally, the New Year came, January 1st, 1932. There was a very noisy celebration in the streets. But in my heart, I felt terrible. Had not that letter caused all these problems, I would have married Feng Zixin that day.

Afterwards, we might have gone to Shanghai and Hangzhou for a honeymoon. Wouldn't that have been nice!

Life is just like playing chess. You make one mistake
and you can lose the whole game.

Chapter Twelve

OUT OF MONEY

ONE DAY, after the three of us had finished our dinner, Lu Deju said we'd better talk about money. I had left all money matters to him. When we began our journey, we had a little over 100 yuan. We had spent 90 yuan already, on the rickshaws, the boat, the hotel, and the sickness. Two days later, we would have to pay the hotel 30 yuan for our second month. But we had only 21 yuan left.

Feng Shujing and I cried out, almost in unison, "Oh, no! What are we going to do?"

Lu Deju said, "I already talked to the front desk manager. For the second month, both of you move into the smaller room, where I'm staying. Every month, you pay only 2 yuan. We just return the big room to the hotel. I will go back home and get some more money, then return. I can bring back some necessities for you. I'll definitely come back before Chinese New Year. The manager agreed. He'll put a portable bed in the hallway for me. He promised to try to find some jobs for you to earn money. As far as food, they'll stop serving you right away. They will let you use a little stove in the room and you can cook by yourself. This will be cheaper."

On January 3, Lu Deju took with him a small amount of money and walked out of the little hotel. Feng Shujing sat in her room, crying. I held his bicycle and walked with him as far as the city gate. He gave me a lot of advice. The most important thing, he said, was that the hotel manager had promised him: if a policeman or some stranger came looking for me, he would try to protect me and let me know, so I could get away. If necessary, the manager would take me to his home temporarily.

When we departed, Lu Deju and I firmly gripped each other's hands. Both of us had tears in our eyes. After a few steps, he turned his head and said, "Write me an express letter if there is some emergency. I can come back any time."

After Lu Deju left, Shujing began to cook meals and wash our clothes. I would go out to buy vegetables, wash the dishes and sweep the floor. Life seemed calm and stable.

Soon after that, the hotel manager found me a job. It was at an elementary school nearby, and my job was primarily to ring the bell for the classes and clean the offices for the school. As pay, I got two silver dollars every month. I thought this was fine. It wouldn't affect my shopping and washing dishes, but it should be enough to pay for the hotel.

The first day on my job, I was very diligent. Some of the teachers looked at me with curious eyes, a worker wearing a gown of fur-lined leather. I was nervous and self-conscious, afraid they would figure out who I was. A young female teacher asked me one day, "Where are you from?" I said, "I'm from downstream." I thought this might be a bad sign. She might have some connection with the police department. I was nervous.

In the afternoon, after I rang the first bell for classes, I started writing a letter to Feng Zixin. I couldn't write the letter at the hotel, so I had to write it at school. I told her how much I missed her, and my heart was always with her. I wanted to figure out a way to find her. I was most worried that Feng Shujing might be pregnant. I was lucky that so far, she wasn't. I hoped God would help me.

One afternoon, after two weeks on the job, after all the teachers had left, when I was cleaning the desks in the office, I began thinking: 'This is really pretty disgusting. I'm in my 20s and I'm being led by my nose by a 16-year-old girl. I gave up my family, almost lost my life, and now I'm cleaning an office in a little school.' The more I thought about it, the more I felt sad and sorry for myself.

Then I noticed there was an organ in one of the classrooms. I hadn't played an organ for a long time. So I opened it up and started playing all the songs I used to know. Suddenly, somebody patted me on the back. I whipped around. It was the vice principal. I stood up, nervously.

"You play really well," he said. "Ever since you came to this school, I figured that you didn't look like a regular worker. Please tell me your true identity. Starting tomorrow, you'll be our new music teacher. Your monthly salary will be 20 yuan."

I told him I was from Shandong and had graduated from Jinan Teacher-Training High School. I thought if I pretended to be from a distant place, that would be too far away to confirm. He was very happy and dragged me to a small restaurant nearby for dinner. He told me the school had been trying for a long time to hire a music teacher, with no luck. Temporarily, the principal's wife was teaching music. She didn't enjoy it, and the students didn't like her. He said, "Now you've solved a big problem for me." As I was leaving, he insisted I take ten meat-filled buns. "Take these to your wife," he said.

I ran home to the hotel. Feng Shujing was having a fit. "Why did you come back so late?" she asked. "Dinner is cold!" Then I took one of the meat buns and stuffed it into her mouth—and told her the good news. She was so happy, she jumped up and down. She took some meat buns to the hotel manager.

The next day, I started teaching my first music class, for sixth graders. I taught them a highly popular song, "Peach Blossom River." They were so excited. After class, some of the students came to me and asked, "Teacher, have you ever been to Shanghai? Did you learn music in Shanghai?" I shook my head. Another student asked me, "Are you still going to ring the class bell today?" I shook my head again, smiling.

Chapter Thirteen

NEWS FROM HOME

WE GOT A LETTER from Lu Deju. He said, "Please try to be frugal. It's really hard to get money. After a few days, I'm going to go to Haizhou and Nancheng and see what's going on there. Before Chinese New Year, I'm going to try to get back to you, and I'll bring some la-rou, dried meat." This was a special Chinese New Year treat.

Lu Deju really made me feel I was deeply indebted to him. I was so touched, I felt like crying. That kind of friendship is beyond imagination. He would go through any kind of hardship and danger to help me. Now it was almost time for Chinese New Year. Instead of spending the holiday season with his wife and children, he would ride his old beat-up bicycle several hundred Chinese miles, to come to this out-of-the-way place and spend the holiday with us. Feng Shujing could be so unreasonable at times, yet when she talked about Lu Deju, she sighed deeply and said, "How did you find such a good friend, who is willing to give his life to you?"

The last day of school before winter vacation, the principal gave a talk in the auditorium. He openly praised me, saying that I was very knowledgeable, very cultured, and a model teacher. After the assembly, I took with me a big package the principal had given to me as a Chinese New Year gift and returned to the hotel.

As I was walking, I thought, 'Tomorrow is Send-off-the-Kitchen-God Day, just a few days before Chinese New Year. So Lu Deju will be arriving soon. When he gets here, we'll have a lot to talk about.'

As I walked in the door, Feng Shujing shouted, "Look who is here!" It was Lu Deju, sitting there eating peanuts. I grabbed his arm and started to cry.

That night, we talked until after 2 a.m. He told me the following few things:

1. The night after we eloped, the Feng family sent out about ten armed men. Five of them went toward Lianyungang, and the other five went to Yangjiaji, in the direction of the Chao River. They didn't find anybody.

2. Feng Shujing's uncle sent someone to my parents' home and to my aunt's home, trying to find out where I was. He was very rude. Of course, he couldn't find out anything because they knew nothing.

3. Both Donghai and Guanyun County governments notified all the nearby towns and villages and piers and river ports, and put both of our names on the 'wanted' list. They

also sent our pictures out with the notice. The government found the negatives in one of the photo studios in Haizhou.

When she heard this, Feng Shujing squeezed my hand and said, "You were right. We probably shouldn't have taken that picture."

4. Huiling's mother, my former wife, had died the previous month. Just before her death, her sister-in-law tried to get her to call out my name. According to local folk beliefs, if she did so, I would die, too. But she shook her head, with tears in her eyes, and refused to call out my name.

5. It was difficult to get money. Lu Deju borrowed some from his cousin, Xu Lupin. He got just enough to buy us some clothing and two pieces of dried meat.

To celebrate the return of Lu Deju and my promotion to become a teacher, Feng Shujing made a lot of dumplings the next day and also cooked a big pork dish. This was the best meal we had eaten since we eloped. We invited the hotel manager to join us and expressed our gratitude. We also gave him a box of New Year cakes (niangao), one of the two given to me by the principal. He was very happy. He said, "All three of you are somebody. You are not common folks."

I asked Lu Deju to take another room at the hotel that night. He refused. He said, "No, money is our lifeline, even more important than life. One day we may need it badly. There may come a day when we may not even have one yuan for all three of our lives, when we are most in need." So he slept in the hallway again, on a cot outside our door.

Everybody was busy that night, celebrating a wonderful New Year's Eve. We made dumplings (shuijiao) and rice balls (yuanxiao), and we cooked the dried meat (la-rou). We also bought several fish, a specialty of Xinghua. Feng Shujing was talking nonstop that night, telling us about her father's bad temper, her mother's tenderness, and how her aunt unabashedly held her husband's hand in front of other people.

Lu Deju said, "That's impossible in our village. It would become a scandal if a woman held a man's hand in public."

Feng Shujing said, "Look what I'm doing!" She was holding my hand.

Lu Deju smiled and said, "You should be ashamed of yourself."

Chapter Fourteen

CAUGHT

AFTER CHINESE NEW YEAR, everything quieted down – except Feng Shujing. She started talking about being homesick. Initially, she just sighed. Later, she started weeping. After a few days, she started to wail, saying, "I have to go home. Otherwise, I can't live." She spoke in almost the same tone she had a few months earlier, when she had said, "If you don't take me away, I can't live."

I was extremely frustrated and bitter. My heart was burning up. I thought, 'Her ideas of 'Let's elope' and 'I'm homesick' are just whatever thoughts come to her mind. Yet she never thinks about the impact on my family, my world, my job, and my life.'

That night, after she went to bed, I started talking to Lu Deju. I told him about my bitter thoughts. He picked up his old erhu, the two-stringed violin. I started to sing "Zhuo Fang Cao," a Chinese opera song about a county magistrate who gave up his position to follow Cao Cao during the Three Kingdoms – and later discovered that Cao Cao was a traitor. The verse I sang was about when the county magistrate, Chen Gong, discovered he had made a mistake. He got stuck in a small hotel, expressing how he regretted what he had done. When I came to this verse, I was so sad, I cried and couldn't continue singing.

Feng Shujing's homesickness got worse every day. Finally, I had no choice but to make plans to take her back home.

In 1932, on January 15th by the Chinese calendar, the celebration of the full-moon festival, we boarded a boat outside Xinghua City. It was a pretty smooth ride. By noon the next day, we arrived at the pier of Funing. Lu Deju disembarked first, pushing his bicycle. We followed behind him.

As we got on the shore, somebody called out, "Feng Shujing!" She inadvertently answered.

Immediately, a policeman arrested us. He was holding our picture in his hand.

I felt as though the whole world had turned upside down. My mouth felt dry. My heart nearly jumped out of my mouth. I looked at Feng Shujing. Her face was like a sheet of white paper. Her lips were trembling.

We were taken to the police station. I thought, 'This is it. Everything is over.'

The police officer did not treat us rudely. He asked us, rather politely, "You both are so young. How did you get so mixed up? If I take you back to the Donghai County seat, you probably both will get a jail term of ten years."

Feng Shujing and I started to beg for his consideration. We used virtually every argument we could think of to persuade him.

The officer never got mad at us. After he thought for a while, he told the policeman who arrested us, "Well, take them away and give them a lecture. As long as they show remorse, just let them go. Give them another chance."

We felt as though we had descended into hell and then climbed out of it.

Feng Shujing kept saying, "Thank you, sir. Thank you, officer."

They took us to a place by the river. One of the policeman said, "You two are very lucky, to meet this particular officer. He himself once had an experience of a free love affair. If you had met an older officer, you both would be finished."

After he stopped talking, he held out his hand to me. I understood immediately. I took out all the money I had with me and gave it to him. He started waving his hand at us again. We took off our watches and gave them to him. He seemed to be satisfied.

Then he said, "That fur-lined leather coat of yours looks good. My father has never worn such a fine coat." I quickly took it off and gave it to him. Underneath, I was wearing only a single-layered cotton scholar's robe. I was shivering. He patted me on the back and said, "You're a smart young man."

Following our arrest, when we were getting the policeman's lecture at the riverside, I noticed that Lu Deju was riding his bicycle in circles nearby. After both policemen left, he flew over and asked, "Are you free to go?"

I nodded, and the three of us cried together.

Chapter Fifteen

RELEASED

FROM THAT PLACE to Lu Deju's home was one full day's walk. Lu said, "We'd better not get into any sort of vehicle or go to a hotel. We cannot walk through any village or town. I know all the back roads in this country." He was also wearing a fur coat. He took off his padded jacket and gave it to me. He carried Feng Shujing on his bicycle, walking ahead. I followed a few hundred yards behind, so people wouldn't see me with her and recognize us.

That evening we stayed in a small Buddhist temple, about five Chinese miles away from Xiangshuikou ("Water-sound-mouth"), Lu Deju's hometown. We had a little money with us because Lu Deju had some, and we shared it with the old monk. After eating some vegetarian food, Lu Deju told us the plan for the next morning.

Feng Shujing grabbed my hand and asked, "After we are separated tomorrow, when can we see each other again?" I pointed to the bright moon in the sky and said,

"Ask her." The whole night I couldn't sleep, but she slept soundly.

Early the next morning, Lu Deju took Feng Shujing to Xiangshuikou, his hometown. I waited for him at the Buddhist temple. Around 10 a.m., he came back.

"I put her in a small hotel and sent a telegram to her family," he said. "By tomorrow, somebody probably will come to pick her up. I paid the hotel and told the hotel manager to watch her and make sure she didn't go out. But when I was leaving, she started crying and begged me to tell you to go see her. I told her you had already left. She cried very hard."

That same afternoon, after sundown, we arrived at Lu Deju's house. It was in a small village by the Chao River. He had a big family, including his parents, his wife, two daughters, five brothers, and more. The house was not very big. Lu Deju told his father about his arrangement. His father said, "I'll go into Xiangshuikou tomorrow. A single girl staying by herself in a hotel, that's not very safe. I'll get another room in the same hotel. I won't even let her know I'm there. But if something happens, I can take care of it. After two days, if her family doesn't pick her up, I'll bring her back."

Nobody said anything, including me. But I was thinking, 'Feng Shujing is such a stubborn, manipulative person. On the other hand, I pity her. Still, if it turns out that she has to come here, to Lu's house, I don't know what I'm going to do.' I had trouble falling asleep that night. At almost daybreak, I started to close my eyes a little.

When I got up, Lu Deju's father had already left. Deju and I were restless the whole day. Right after sundown, the old gentleman came home. As he walked in the door, he was smiling. "Everything went smoothly," he said. "I saw her get into a rickshaw. There were two armed guards on bicycles with her."

I thought, 'Whew. Finally this terrible, ugly, dangerous drama has ended.'

I stayed with the Lu family for about a week. I sent a letter to my family and told them I was safe. I also sent a letter to a cousin of mine, who was teaching at a nearby school, and asked him to meet me at the Lu house. Also, I sent five letters to Feng Zixin and asked her to send her responses to my parents' house in Nancheng.

The conditions of the Lu family were not very good. The old man had once been the principal of the Xiangshuikou Elementary School. After Lu Deju graduated from the Teacher-Training School, he also taught at that school for a few years, but both of them were unemployed by this time. They had a few acres of wheat fields. Of the annual harvest, two thirds were used for the family's food supply and one third was sold to cover the family expenses. One of the largest expenses was the old man's liquor. Every day he had to have three drinks; he couldn't miss even one.

After my cousin came, I said goodbye to the Lu family. After that, I stayed with my cousin at his school. After a few days, I asked my cousin to go back to Nancheng to find out the situation after Feng Shujing went home. Also, I asked him to tell my parents I needed to quickly go to the South. I could not stay in my hometown. Also, if there were letters for me, I asked him to bring them back.

After my cousin left, I worked as a substitute teacher, teaching in his place. The whole school had only 70 students. They had two classrooms: one for first and second grade, and the other for third and fourth grade. Every day, they had six classes. The principal and my cousin each handled one classroom. The principal's wife took care of all the rest of the work at the school, miscellaneous things such as cooking dinner and washing clothes.

Besides teaching every day, I spent some time walking near the school. It was in a remote village, with a lot of vegetation and trees; people were simple but nice. When I had left the Lu home, Lu Deju had put a bunch of coins in my pocket. With one dime, I could buy a whole bunch of peanuts. I would sit under a tree, eating peanuts and thinking over the experiences of the previous few months.

Some days had passed like a light breeze and others like a thunderstorm. Sometimes I had felt like I was sipping delicate tea, and other times I had been drinking bitter wine. Overall, I couldn't judge whether it had been sweet or bitter, whether it was pleasant reality or a bad dream.

Chapter Sixteen

HOME

AFTER FOUR DAYS, my cousin came back. Here's what he told me:

After Feng Shujing returned home, the local paper ran an article about it, and the Feng family indicated that everything was over. They would not take any further action against me. The article said I had already left the area and gone to the South.

However, the brother of the principal of my junior high school was working for a small newspaper in Shanghai. He said he would do everything he could to try to find me and kill me.

My father, because of economic hardship, had gone to Xinpu before Chinese New Year and got into a joint venture with another man to open up a salted fish store. But the business was very poor, and everybody in my family could eat only rice gruel and sweet potatoes.

Also, my cousin brought back two pairs of socks, two sets of underwear, and an old padded cotton jacket, from my mother. There were also two letters: one from my uncle sent to my father. In it, he scolded me badly and also mentioned my great uncle, Santaiye, saying, "Great Uncle is furious. He plans to take Ping-Nan to the family temple and have him judged according to the family law."

The second letter was not from Feng Zixin. It was from Feng Shujing. She said, "After I got home, my parents were very, very happy that I was safe. They do not hate you. They asked me to tell you that if you can get a matchmaker to come to them, they will agree to our marriage. How would you like that? They asked me where you were. I said you had probably gone south after staying in Xiangshuikou."

But I never received a letter from Feng Zixin. After I had left Lu's home, I sent her a couple more letters. I suspected that she didn't want to forgive me. I hoped I would have a chance to explain it to her when I saw her in person.

By early February according to the Chinese calendar, I couldn't wait any longer. In the dark of night, I returned to Nancheng. I went to the back entrance of my family's courtyard and knocked on the wooden door.

My mother opened it. She immediately began to cry.

Chapter Seventeen

CHEATED

I HID AT HOME for two days. Then I went to Xinpu to visit my father at the salted fish store. It stank. The following day, my father went to a shop and bought some things for me. He bumped into a man named Chou Peisheng, who was one of my classmates at the No. 8 Teacher-Training High School, and he was a Kuomintang Party official. At the time, he was unemployed, preparing to go to Zhenjiang to look for a job. My father always thought very highly of him. He begged him to take me with him. He agreed.

After two days, Chou Peisheng and I got on the train together. My father gave him 40 silver dollars. That money was supposed to be my whole life support. When the train passed Xiaguan, near Nanjing, I wanted to get off and go to Nanjing to look for Feng Zixin, but he didn't agree. He said the hotels in Nanjing were very expensive and it was hard to find jobs.

"There's no hurry to look for that girl of yours. Why don't you go to Zhenjiang with me? I'll help you find a job."

I didn't have much choice. So I did.

Chou Peisheng's wife was waiting for him at the train station. She was middle-aged, fat and ugly. She didn't even say hello to me. We went to a hotel, and they went inside the room and closed the door. They made me stay outside, in the hallway. I knocked on the door and asked him to give me the money.

"I'll talk to you tomorrow," he said. Then he threw a quilt out to me. So I had to sleep in the hallway. The next morning, they went out without talking to me. My stomach was empty. I waited till evening, and they didn't come back. I asked the innkeeper, and he told me that Mr. Chou had already left for Shanghai.

"It looks like he left with your money," he said.

Forty silver dollars. My livelihood. Gone. I had nothing.

The innkeeper was sympathetic. "Well, maybe I'll see what I can do tomorrow," he said. It happened that this innkeeper came from the same hometown, so he was willing to look out for me.

This fellow went out in the morning and came back about noon. With him was a cousin of mine named Wu Linqing and a man named Gao. They asked, "Have you eaten?"

"For three days, I've eaten very little," I said. They bought me a meal and I told them about my experiences.

Wu Linqing said, "It looks like the old fox did it again. He's a bad man."

Mr. Gao, the other man at the lunch, was also from the Lianyungang area. His brother was a fairly high-ranking military man, and Mr. Gao was working in the army as an accountant. He seemed to be living a comfortable life. After lunch, he said, "After listening to your story, although this is our first time meeting each other, I can see you are a nice young man. Why don't you work for me temporarily, and I'll take care of your room and board. I will pay you 14 silver dollars each month as pocket money."

I thanked him profusely.

My cousin, Linqing, patted me on the back and said, "You're a lucky guy. One word from Mr. Gao and all your problems are solved! This afternoon, why don't we go to Yangzhou together." That was where his wife and their daughter, Qiangmin, were. I found out later that my cousin Linqing was also unemployed. He was temporarily staying with his aunt in Nanjing.

Yangzhou is a very pretty city, with a lake known as "Narrow West Lake." Centuries ago, Emperor Qianlong went there and stayed for a long time and refused to leave. Now I know why. Linqing had a cousin who used to be one of my students at Guanyun County School. During my stay in Yangzhou, he often took me out boating on the lake, to local theater performances, and to many different restaurants. We saw many pretty young women there.

But Wu Linqing's wife complained to me sometimes, saying, "You made such a big fuss about wanting to get a divorce. Now Wu Linqing is talking about divorcing me!" When she said that, she was crying, with tears coming out of her eyes. In her arms, she was holding Qiangmin, who was barely two years old. I felt terrible.

After staying in Yangzhou for three days, I returned to Zhenjiang and took up my job. Zhenjiang is south of the Yangtze River and was then the capital of Jiangsu Province. I did some work for the army commander, writing several letters for him and preparing a couple of speeches.

Then I started writing to Feng Zixin. But I did not receive any reply. I was thinking of going to Nanjing to look her up, but I hesitated. I knew that Feng Zixin had a fiery temperament. Plus, she had good reason to be angry with me.

Chapter Eighteen

A LONG SHOT

ONE DAY, Linqing came over with a newspaper article, which he showed me. It was an announcement saying that the Central Military Academy in Nanjing was inviting applications for a training program for 'special military commissars' – for Kuomintang political officers to be attached to the military troops.

The primary qualification required was a bachelor's degree from a university. The entrance examination would include Chinese literature, Sun Yat-sen's Three Principles of the People, political science, economics, sociology, psychology, history, and geography. Also, there would be three interviews.

When I read that, I shook my head. I had never even attended university, let alone graduated.

"You should be courageous enough to try for it," Linqing said.

"But I don't have a college degree," I replied.

Mr. Gao heard our discussion. "I can take care of that. I know a way to get you a fake diploma."

That might make it at least possible to take the exam. But other than Chinese literature, I had no knowledge of these topics.

"Don't worry," said Mr. Gao. "I'll go to the library and get out books for you to study. With your intelligence, if you put in some extra hard work over the next two and a half months, I believe you really have a good shot at this."

In addition to Mr. Gao, I was encouraged by a friend of Wu Linqing's called Mr. Xia, who decided that he would also take the examination and apply for this program. He was a recent graduate of the famous National University of Law and Politics. In that city, he was well-known as an extremely brilliant young man.

The following day, Linqing brought me a big suitcase full of books. Mr. Gao arranged a special room in the back for me to study. He said, "Within the next two and a half months, you don't have to do anything but study. Next month, I'm going to go to Nanjing for a conference. I want two photos of you and a summary of your life. I will make sure to get the application in order. The rest is up to you."

That afternoon, Mr. Xia left, too, returning to Lianyungang. Before leaving, he said, in all seriousness, "I'll see you in Nanjing."

From that day on, I buried my head in the books. I tried to read as much as possible every day, and I took very careful notes. I got up at five o'clock every morning. Normally, I didn't go to bed until midnight. During those

19 hours, I took a break three times a day, only for meals. I did not waste one minute.

The first few days, I felt a little dizzy. After that, I felt I was making good progress every day, learning a lot. Also, my self-confidence seemed to grow stronger daily.

After a month, Mr. Gao came back from Nanjing with a completed application form, including an admission ticket for the examination. He told me, "It's my understanding that the Kuomintang and the military academy want to train a group of cadres for eventual leadership positions. This is the purpose of establishing this program. They will accept only 500 people. Among the 500 who are accepted, 400 will be selected from all college graduates who apply. The other 100 will be selected by President Chiang Kai-Shek from among men who have graduated from the military academy these last six years, the first six graduating classes. Already, more than one thousand people have applied for the 400 open positions."

My ticket number was 926.

Chapter Nineteen

LAST TOSS OF THE DICE

DURING THOSE TWO MONTHS of preparation, I finished reading all the books I was supposed to read. I spent another week reviewing everything I'd read.

At the last moment, I suddenly received a letter from Feng Zixin. My trembling hands opened the letter. She started by saying, "I have received all of the 40-some letters you wrote to me. I was angry at first. But then I began to sympathize with the difficulties you had, the risks you took, and the danger you faced. I have often thought of replying to your letters. Sometimes I even had the urge to see you. But I could never bring myself to do that. I was afraid that if I wrote to you or saw you, it would cause more damage to both of us."

Her letter continued, saying: "First, you said my cousin, Feng Shujing, threatened you with suicide in order to get you to elope with her. Her ultimate weapon was the five letters I wrote. But if she had really publicized those five letters and then killed herself, neither you nor I would have had any legal responsibility, would we?

Of course, if she had evidence of something else you did, something I don't know about, she could have used that as leverage.

"Second, do you remember, after your divorce was final, how happy we were, holding each other? We swore seriously to each other that you would never be close to another woman, and I would never touch another man as long as we both lived. So how can you explain this to me? Do you still love me? Do I still love you? I have many, many questions that don't have answers."

After reading this letter, I felt like a knife had stabbed my heart. I was sweating cold sweat. All the things I read over the last two months seemed to fly out of my head, and my mind was empty. Nothing was left except the question marks in Feng Zixin's letter.

That night, I could not sleep at all. At daybreak, I made two decisions. First, I would put aside the letter from Feng Zixin and deal with it later. Second, I needed to concentrate on my studying. There were only two more weeks before the examination. This was my last chance to make something of my life.

I felt like a gambler with nothing left but this last toss of the dice. If I won, I would have a good future. If I lost, I might as well just jump into the Yangtze River as my final answer to Feng Zixin's letter.

After this decision, I felt calmer. I spent another week studying hard. I began to have a good idea of the core of every subject. Toward the end, I began to believe that Mr. Gao was right: I should have a fairly good shot at this examination.

I received a letter from Mr. Xia. He asked me to meet him in Nanjing three days later, at the home of a friend of his, a man named Mr. Sun. Mr. Sun was also a graduate of the No. 8 Teacher-Training School. At the time, he was working at a bank in Nanjing. He was a very generous man. I received a letter from him the next day, inviting me to stay with him when I came to Nanjing to take the exam. So Mr. Xia and I both stayed at Mr. Sun's house. He was a very well-to-do man, with a nice big house.

Mr. Xia appeared to have lost some weight, perhaps because of the hard work he put in over the last few months, studying.

The first thing he told me was that he had already checked out the situation. There were more than 3,000 applicants for the 400 openings. More than twenty of the 3,000 had degrees from overseas universities. "Everybody sees this as the opportunity of a lifetime," he said.

Originally, I had felt confident that I would be admitted with the highest ranking. Now, after hearing this, I was honestly scared. To achieve one of the top 400 scores would be even harder than I had imagined. I was no longer sure I could do it.

On the third day, we started the exam. It took three full days. I felt I was fairly cool. I didn't panic. Any opportunity I got, I always tried to express myself as fully as possible. One question was: "Explain the reasons for Napoleon's defeat." I wrote an essay of about 5,000 words.

After the written exam, I had to undergo a series of personal interviews. The last one was conducted by the head of the military academy, Lt. General Liu. He asked me one question: "Who are the most valuable people in our society?"

I replied, "Those who participate in production."

He nodded and smiled at me. I felt very encouraged.

We waited two weeks for the announcement of the results. Each day felt like a year. Mr. Xia spent most of his time at the mahjongg table.

One day, during lunch, he said to me, "This time, for this examination, I don't think I'll have any problem passing. But for you, I think it would be very difficult. I know of an opening for an elementary school teacher across the river from Nanjing. Are you interested in that job?"

I shook my head and did not reply. Afterwards, I went to one of Nanjing's most famous sites, the tombs of the Ming emperors, for a walk, just thinking.

Finally, the date of the announcement came. We found out that the names of those who had been selected would be posted in front of the office of the Department of Political Affairs of the armed forces. I got up very early that day, but I was a little timid about going to see the announcement. As I hesitated, Mr. Xia walked confidently toward the door and waved at me, saying, "I'm going to look at the announcement. You don't have to go. If you don't find your name there, it will be very difficult."

In a way, I took it for granted that I probably would not be admitted. After all, I did not have a college education. Still, I wanted it badly. I had studied so hard. I was very nervous, and my mind was spinning.

After a while I heard Mr. Xia come back. He was screaming, "This government is going to be overthrown! I don't understand how this could happen. How could they reject a man with my qualifications, with my ability!"

Mr. Sun and I walked toward him. I knew that if he couldn't get in, definitely I would not have a chance. All that studying, all that hope –wasted. Now what would I do?

He was foaming at the mouth and cursing. Then he grabbed my hand. He said: "You are like a blind cat that caught a live mouse. You got in! And your ranking is fairly high."

A wave of dizziness washed over my head, as if I had been drinking. Mr. Sun congratulated me and said: "You should be happy now. Why are you crying?"

Stunned, I quietly walked out the door and went to Mingwalang, where they had posted the announcement. There were a lot of people there, crowding around, trying to get in close and read the postings.

I managed to elbow my way to the front so I could see. I was astounded to find out that my name was listed as number 26. Twenty-six!

I scanned through all the names to make sure I wouldn't miss Mr. Xia's name, but I couldn't find his name on the list.

Then I returned to Mr. Sun's house in Xin Jiekou, where I was staying. I wrote a letter to my father and also letters to Lu Deju, to my great uncle Santaiye, and to my cousin Wu Linqing with the good news. I mailed the letters by express mail. The hardest letter to write was the one to Feng Zixin.

In the evening, when Mr. Sun came back from work, he took me to dinner at a small restaurant nearby. I was so happy that I had two cups of Shaoxing wine. I even got a little drunk. After returning to my room, I quickly went to sleep.

When I woke up in the middle of the night, it was raining outside. I began to think about all the frightening events of the past year. Emotions swept through me and I felt out of control.

I thought of the famous poem: "Tears and rain." It goes like this: "On the other side of my window, I listen to the rain as it beats on the window until daybreak." I couldn't remember who wrote the poem, but it described precisely how I felt at the time.

The next morning, I got up very late. I searched through my pockets and found I had a few dollars left. Braving the rain, I went to the street and bought some stationery and stamps, as well as a needle and thread and some buttons.

I also bought a pipe and tobacco for Lu Deju's father. The last time I had seen him, he was using small pipe of the type made by farmers, which didn't look very nice. I hoped he would like the new pipe I sent to him.

Chapter Twenty

PLEA FOR A SECOND CHANCE

THAT NIGHT, I couldn't go to sleep, so I got up and started writing a letter to Feng Zixin.

"As luck would have it," my letter began, "I was admitted to the Chinese Military Academy political department. I have to report to school on July 1. I'm not writing you just because I just received this happy news. On the contrary. If I hadn't been admitted, I would write you anyway. But that letter would have been my last will and testament. Because I had decided, if I couldn't make it in to the school, there would be no room for me in this world.

"During the last year, when you did not respond to my letters, you terminated my last thread of desire to live. I had no more hope. The only option I could imagine, to seek my ultimate relief, was to jump into the Yangtze River. Finally, in Zhenjiang, I received one letter from you. To me, it felt like a declaration of execution.

"If you find it in your heart to allow this condemned man one more chance to explain himself, please consider the following two points of my rather foolish explanation.

"I did consider the possibility that Feng Shujing's threat to kill herself might not be entirely true. But in case she did carry out her threat, leaving a letter accusing me, she would be gone forever, and how could I ever explain my innocence to anyone? I would never have a chance to explain myself. Besides, if she made public the five letters from you that she stole, everyone could read the letters in which you urged me to get a divorce and began planning our marriage. This would make it appear that you manipulated my divorce, and you might be accused of criminal responsibility.

"I certainly did not forget—and will never forget—what we promised each other. But please consider: If you were in my shoes, would you have been able to prevent this outcome?

"Now we have to face it. I was young, and I'm not superhuman. I'm subject to temptations just like anyone else. But I have always tried to be truthful to you. I hope, I pray, that you will forgive me this once for being such a pitiful, half-drowned cur.

"As for the three questions you asked of me, I think I'm qualified. What I can say with a clear mind, and totally without regret, is this: I still love you just as I did before. Maybe more, because now I feel I owe you so much."

After I sent this letter out, I felt much relieved. At least she would know how I felt.

It was a long shot, hoping that she might forgive me and take me back. But so was my acceptance into the military academy. Perhaps my luck had turned.

Chapter Twenty-One

MILITARY LIFE

I REPORTED to the military academy on July 1st. That day, I picked up my uniform, my toiletries, and my daily necessities. Then we all had to shave our heads.

Looking back, I recall that I shaved my head three times during my life. The first time was when I was very little. When I went to the Buddhist monastery, they insisted on shaving my head. The second time was when I entered the No. 8 Teacher-Training School. This was the third time.

I was assigned to the second battalion. Our commander told us that our military academy training would last for one year. We would be paid a monthly stipend of 14 silver dollars, plus free meals. Every Saturday night, we could take leave from 7 p.m. until 10 p.m. On Sundays, we were permitted to stay out all day, between 6 a.m. and 10 p.m.

I thought this was not a bad life, compared to what I went through in that little hotel in Xinghua.

Every day, we had four hours of military drill. Then we had four hours in the classroom, followed by a two-hour study period. It was very taxing physically. I always felt hungry. I always felt like I didn't get enough sleep. But every time I went to bed, I thought about Feng Zixin.

After a week in the academy, I couldn't stand it any more, not hearing from her. So I wrote her another letter.

"This Saturday night, between 7:00 and 9:30 p.m.," I wrote, "I will be waiting for you in the pagoda of the No. 1 Park. If you don't come, I will wait for you every Saturday, at the same time and place, rain or shine. Some day, I believe, you will show up."

Chapter Twenty-Two

TEARS AND RAIN

THAT SATURDAY, it was raining very hard. At 7:00, my heart started to pound. I went to the park and found the pagoda. The rain got heavier and heavier. I couldn't see anyone else in the park. By the street light, I looked at my watch and read 8 p.m.

Feng Zixin suddenly flew into my arms, like a bird. She felt like a lonely child who just returned home into her mother's arms, weeping inconsolably. I held her tight. She cried harder. We sat on a stone bench. She sat on my lap and I put my arms around her. Water was flowing down from hair, dripping on her shoulders. I couldn't tell whether it was her tears or rain.

"You look thinner," I said.

She cried even harder. I thought of the poem in Dream of the Red Chamber, which says, "I was so dizzy I couldn't get out of bed. I was sick because of missing my lover, but I was ashamed by my love."

After a long while, she could finally speak. "I read your letter many times," she said. "I guess I cannot disagree with you. Rationally, I ought to forgive you. But subconsciously, I suspect my wounds are so deep I could never sew them up." She started crying again. "Over the last few months, every time I thought about you and Feng Shujing, my whole body trembled. I often told myself, I wish I had never met you. That would be so much better."

I listened to everything she had to say. Then I said, "Let's not mention Feng Shujing's name any more in our whole life." Finally, I kissed her on her lips.

After this, we regularly met at the same place on Saturday evenings, and on Sundays we often went to the Ming Tombs or Xuanwu Lake Park for a picnic. She usually appeared to be happy. But sometimes she would suddenly bite me on my arm or leg very hard, sometimes even drawing blood. I understood what she meant. It didn't hurt. But I deserved it. I told myself, this is my punishment.

Chapter Twenty-Three

FATEFUL CHOICE

ORIGINALLY, MY CLASS WAS supposed to graduate from the military academy on June 30, 1933. But because the Japanese army invaded northeast China, Manchuria, as far as the Great Wall and the military situation got very tense, the academy decided to move our graduation date to March 29, which is the anniversary of Huanghua Gang, a major event in Sun Yatsen's revolutionary uprising. The army needed us to get to work.

The academy surprised me with my first assignment. They asked me to go to Shanghai to join the Nuchao Angry Storm Theatrical Troupe, a group that later became part of Lianhua Movie Studios. I was assigned to work with them as a playwright, to develop anti-Japanese propaganda plays. I would not be on the front line, but I would be doing the vital work of building public support for the war effort. To me, this seemed like an ideal job, important yet safe.

Feng Zixin was thrilled. Shanghai was not too far from Nanjing by train, and I would not be in danger.

Once she finished nursing school, she hoped to join me there.

As it happens, though, I didn't go. One of my classmates, Wang Jianhun, got hold of me. He gave me a stern lecture and even yelled at me, saying, "I didn't realize you were such a coward! The Japanese are swallowing up Manchuria. They have just started shelling our troops with their cannons on the Great Wall. Are you afraid to go to the front line and shed blood for your country? You'd rather go to decadent Shanghai and join this senseless lowlife theatrical troupe? How can you call yourself Chinese?"

He was almost in tears when he talked to me. I was really moved.

I guess I did have a strong sense of loyalty to my country. On top of that, I had always had a strong hatred of the Japanese invaders attacking China.

Another important factor: If I went to Shanghai, it would definitely seal my marriage with Feng Zixin. That made me nervous. How could I be sure that, after marriage, her subconscious anger wouldn't emerge and poison our relationship? If I put on the brakes at this point, I would always have the memory of this perfect love, forever.

Therefore, I decided to go with my friend Mr. Wang to see the head of our military academy, Liu Jianchun. With a heavy heart, I requested that I be reassigned to the 40th Army in Northern China.

This decision changed my whole life, sending me in a new direction for both my personal life and my career.

The next time I saw Feng Zixin, we met at the same pagoda in Nanjing's Number 1 Park and sat on the same stone bench. Once again, it was raining, this time a dull, steady downpour. Clouds covered the moon.

I told her that I had been re-assigned. The army needed me to go to the North, near the Great Wall, to join the fight against the Japanese invaders.

She was shocked. "How could they change their minds so quickly?"

I didn't tell her the whole story. I just explained that I had no choice. The decision was final. Manchuria had already been occupied by Japanese troops, and they were threatening to come over the Wall to invade northern China. Every Chinese had an obligation to do our utmost to protect our country from invasion. The military had trained me to be a political commissar to the army, and they needed me in the North.

She wept uncontrollably. She no longer felt like a bird in my arms, or like a pail of gasoline. Instead, she felt like a wet towel, draping over my arms.

"When you were assigned to go to Shanghai, I tasted hope, for the first time in a year. I began imagining our future life together," she said. "Now I know it was a cruel illusion."

"It's not up to me," I told her. "Besides, in times like these, how could I go to Shanghai?"

"You never really tried to make it work between us," she said. But that wasn't true. I had come to Nanjing, and I had tried. But the trust was gone.

"I'll write to you," I said.

"I want three letters a day," she said, with a sad smile.

"After the war is over, maybe we can be together always," I said.

She shook her head. She knew better than to hope. And I didn't have the heart to make a promise I couldn't keep.

"Who can know the future?" I said.

Feng Zixin and I spent the whole night together in that pagoda, holding on to each other, and saying good-bye.

The next morning, the rain had stopped. I woke up in her arms.

She hadn't slept at all. She kissed me, hard, then stood up.

"I've been thinking," she said. "If I can't love you for my whole life, I'll just have to hate you for my whole life. Because I can't forget you for my whole life."

Then she walked away, swaying slightly in the pale light of dawn.

The day I left Nanjing, she came to the train station to see me off. Her beautiful eyes were crumpled with tears. I wanted to feel proud and patriotic, but instead my heart ached at the death of a dream.

I was born like a wild horse. It was very hard to tame me. Feng Zixin tried to control me with a metal chain; at times it felt like a fire burning and at times we were bleeding and crying. She managed to excite my senses and set my soul aflame, but she could not control me.

Part II

THE WAR YEARS

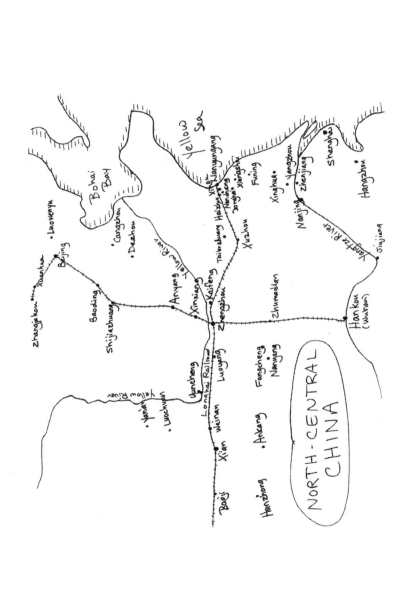

Chapter Twenty-Four

CHILL WINDS ON
THE GREAT WALL

IN THE EARLY SPRING, with a chill wind blowing over North China's empty horizon, we bumped along dirt roads in an army truck and arrived near the Great Wall, an area called Luowenyu. There we reported to the 40th Army. I led a group of six men, including Wang Jianhun. We were assigned to 115th regiment of the second battalion of China's national army.

When we graduated, the Central Military Commission officially gave us military ranking. I was given the ranking of zhongxiao, lieutenant colonel. Of all the classmates in our graduating class, only ten got this ranking. Most of the others got major or captain. My official title at that time was Lt. Col. Yang Ping-Nan, Secretary of the Political Commissar Department of the 40th Army. In the same group, Wang Jianhun, Peng Hongwen, and Dai Zhongyu were given the ranking of major (xiaoxiao).

At first, I was assigned not to the 40th Army's central headquarters but to a battalion commander, a man named Zhu Jialin. Commander Zhu asked me to give an early morning pep talk to the soldiers and officers, every day after we raised the flag, for thirty minutes. So every morning, I spoke to them, repeating everything I learned in the academy.

The Japanese army was camped on the other side of the Great Wall. Sometimes we would exchange fire with artillery or with rifles. But it was more like a symbolic war. After a while, it became quiet.

I had been sent by the Chinese Army, under Chiang Kai-Shek, to serve as a political commissar to the 40th Army, which was under the overall command of General Pang Bingxun. My job was to let Chiang Kai-Shek and his military know what was going on, since General Pang had only recently joined the Nationalist cause. In earlier years, he had been a military officer under Feng Yuxiang, a powerful warlord in northern China. I was to be the eyes and ears of the national government, reporting any possible signs of disloyalty. When I sent my reports back to Nanjing, I wrote in rice soup on paper so that no one else could read my reports. In Nanjing, my military superiors used a special chemical to make my writing reappear.

Zhu Jialin

Zhu Jialin was an impressive man. Originally from a village in Hebei, he had graduated from Baoding Military Academy, in the eighth graduating class, specializing in artillery. He was in the same class and same regiment as Chen Cheng, one of Chiang Kai-Shek's top generals. He was very strict with his troops. If any of his high level subordinates stepped out of line, he would slap them in the face. He demanded a high level of discipline and he always set an example himself.

Commander Zhu seemed to like me very much. He was very kind to me. Often, he would invite me to his room just to chat. Sometimes he even talked about his family. At one point, he asked me: "Are you married?"

I said, "I did marry once. But because she was illiterate—she could not read even a single character—we couldn't get along, so we got divorced."

My office was always right next to the regiment commander's office. One day Commander Zhu was in my office and we were talking about something when a soldier came in with a letter for me. Actually, it was a book sent to me from Shanghai by Feng Zixin. The book was a translation of a book by a foreign author, with a title translated as "The Troubles of Young Werther."

Commander Zhu saw the book and asked, "Who is Young Werther?"

"He's a German," I said.

"What are his troubles?"

"Trouble with women," I answered.

After that he just left the room.

That package included a letter from Feng Zixin, saying that she was moving. She did not give me her new address. "This will be my last letter," she wrote. "I get it now. It will never work between us. Please don't try to find me."

She had a flair for the dramatic. But in fact, after that, her letters stopped.

One day, Commander Zhu told me the government had just signed an agreement called the Tanggu Accord. "Tonight we can retreat to a different location."

Before we decamped, Mr. Zhu assigned me a horse. The rest of my classmates had to walk with the soldiers.

The 40th Army moved to a suburb of Beijing called Tongzhou. We stayed there for one month. At that time, Feng Yuxiang, the warlord who controlled much of North China, declared independence in Zhangjiakou and organized an independent government. This was a terrible blow to Chiang Kai-Shek and the national army, which had worked hard to create an alliance with him.

Chiang Kai-Shek responded by appointing General Pang Bingxun, the head of the 40th Army, to become the governor of Chahar Province, north of Hebei. That was a tempting and potentially powerful position, but first General Pang had to win back control of Chahar Province. He was ordered to lead the 40th Army to Zhangjiakou to fight against the army of Feng Yuxiang, his former boss. So our army began moving toward the west along the Beijing-Suiyuan Railroad. Midway, we passed through a small city called Shacheng.

In southern China, Chen Mingqu, a warlord in Fujian, also staged a military coup. China's central government was not strong enough to ensure the loyalty of these warlords who had once agreed to be its allies.

At that time, General Pang assigned me to prepare two telegrams, one to openly condemn Chen Mingqu and another to condemn Feng Yuxiang. He needed to reassure the central government of his own continued loyalty. General Pang was very pleased with my work. Therefore, he immediately transferred me to his own office staff, to serve at the headquarters of 40th Army's overall commander.

General Pang also told me in person, "When I get to Zhangjiakou and become the governor, I'll appoint you as county executive of Xuanhua County in Chahar." Those were heady words, because county executives were powerful local government officials. But his promise didn't mean anything because we didn't have control of Chahar yet. I moved to General Pang's office, and my friend Wang took over my job with battalion commander Zhu Jialin. Wang got along very well with Commander Zhu.

When our army arrived in Xuanhua, which was a major city, we confronted Feng Yuxiang's army. The confrontation went on for almost half a year. There was no major progress either way. Because General Pang used to serve under Feng Yuxiang, as one of his subordinates, he felt uncomfortable fighting him directly with his army. This was obvious to everyone, but of course General Pang would not admit it.

The warlord Feng Yuxiang was very smart and cunning. He said, "Pang Bingxun, you can come here and become my governor instead. I will become one of your subjects." Pang Bingxun did not accept this offer to defect, but he also could not give his troops the order to engage in a heavy fire fight. Feng Yuxiang had a bigger, more powerful army, and he refused to leave Zhangjiakou.

This stalemated confrontation went on until the spring of 1934. Chiang Kai-Shek was furious about it but could do nothing. Finally, Chiang Kai-Shek sent the governor of Shandong Province, Han Fuqu, to invite Feng Yuxiang to Mount Tai for a vacation. To everyone's amazement, he went. In the meantime, Chiang Kai-Shek sent Song Zheyuan, a trusted high general in the national army, to replace Pang Bingxun as governor of Chahar. He moved Pang Bingxun and his army to Nanyang in Henan Province for reorganization and training.

When I got on the train leaving Xuanhua, I was thinking, there goes my job as Xuanhua county executive!

Chapter Twenty-Five

THE RIGHT CHOICE

THE DAY WE ARRIVED in Nanyang was the one year anniversary of my graduation from the academy.

At that time, the political commissar department needed a captain who could teach military songs to the soldiers and officers. I recommended to my boss that Lu Deju be hired to do that. He was still teaching school in Nancheng. My boss, Chen Chunlin, the head of the Political Commissar Department, agreed. I was very happy. At that time, a teacher-training college graduate who came to our army could get only an initial ranking of sergeant. In fact, Lu Deju hadn't even graduated from college. He had just graduated from a teacher-training high school. I sent a letter to him by express mail. I also attached 20 yuan for travel expenses. In about a week, he came to report for his job.

When he arrived, we talked for the whole night. He told me he had visited my home, where he found out that I had been sending money to my parents. He told me their life seemed to be much improved. Most of the debts had been paid off. My father had closed the salted fish store. Often he played mahjongg.

I asked Lu Deju if he heard any news about Feng Shujing. He said he heard she married an officer of the army stationed in the area. I was glad to hear this. He had not heard any news about Feng Zixin; she seemed to have disappeared. I was no longer getting letters from her.

Lu Deju also told me that his father liked the pipe I sent him very much. He always had it in his mouth. I was glad I could do something to repay the kindness his family had shown to me when my life was in disarray.

In 1934, on January 15th according to the lunar calendar, the 40th army, still under Pang Bingxun, was ordered to go to the Ankang area of Shaanxi Province to fight against the Communists. Just after we started the journey, it began to snow. The air was frigid, and the roads were icy and slippery. Even riding on a horse, traveling was tough. After two days, we got into the mountainous area. We couldn't ride our horses, so we all had to walk. We walked for eleven days before arriving at Ankang. Soon after that, my boss, Mr. Chen, returned to Nanjing and I was appointed to replace him as head of the commissar department for the whole 40th Army. Suddenly I became a colonel (shangxiao), after less than two years of service.

General Pang did not bring his family with him during this move, so he often asked me to go hunting with him. Often he shot rabbits and after hunting, we ate rabbit meat. To me, this was a burden, but a lot of people were envious of me. Even the deputy commander felt this way. One day, I overheard the deputy commander say, "If any of you men needs something from Mr. Pang, the best person to ask is Mr. Yang." Indeed, Mr. Pang trusted me very much. Whatever I suggested, he always seemed to follow.

One of my colleagues hinted to me that Mr. Pang might be considering having his oldest daughter marry me. If I agreed, he might send me to a foreign country to study. This was like a feeler, to see what I thought of this probability. I tactfully said no. I had seen Mr. Pang's family photo, and I remembered that his daughter looked like him, short and fat.

I said, "No thanks. I am just not prepared to make this kind of commitment." Also I knew it would not be a good idea for me to marry the daughter of the Commanding General—not good for either of us. My job as head commissar required that I watch over the commanding general on behalf of the central government. How could I do this if I was married to his daughter? It would be seen as a conflict of interest.

At that time, another couple of colleagues also tried to fix me up with another woman. I had no interest at that time. I was still recovering from the wounds of my relationships with the two Feng girls.

During those months, I was very busy with my work and I wasn't really interested in finding a wife and settling down. Soon Li Jishen, another warlord in the south, in

Fujian, rebelled against the Central Government, so the general asked me to prepare a denunciation telegram to be sent and also published. He asked several people to draft such a telegram. After he looked over four or five versions, he said he liked the version I prepared. That was published right away, in all the newspapers the next day. It was widely praised by several major newspapers. Chiang Kai-Shek even sent a telegram to General Pang, expressing appreciation for his support. After all this, General Pang was very happy, always rubbing his beard and saying, "Yang Ping-Nan is really a genius." After that, everybody called me a genius.

The camp of No. 2 Battalion, under Commander Zhu Jialin, was rather far from the general's quarters, where I stayed. But one day, Wang Jianhun sent me a wireless telegram, saying that he was sending a messenger with a letter and asking me to please send my reply to him, through this messenger. I could not figure out what this was about.

A week later, the messenger arrived. He handed me the letter from Wang Jianhun. I opened it, and two pictures slipped out of the envelope. I looked at the pictures, which showed a pretty young lady. She had exactly the same eyes and nose as Feng Zixin and wore a white blouse, a black skirt, and athletic shoes, with a very simple straight haircut. I vividly recalled the image of Feng Zixin. After my initial surprise, I started reading Wang Jianhun's letter.

He wrote, "You are very foolish man. You can never forget that little girl who was crying at the Nanjing train station, seeing you off when we left for the Great Wall, can you? Battalion Commander Zhu Jialin likes you very much. As you recall, he normally keeps a straight face. But any time he mentions your name, he starts to smile. This is fate. He wants you to marry his most beloved daughter, Zhu Bingwen. Here are two recent photos. She is now in her second year of high school in Baoding. Please don't disappoint Commander Zhu. Give your reply to the messenger and also send us a recent photo of yourself. Also include your birth date and time. Her mother wants to have a fortune-teller look at your birth date and calculate what kind of life you'll have in the future."

I told the messenger to come back and pick up my reply at 7 a.m. the next morning. All night, I thought about this, long and hard. I thought about Feng Zixin constantly, but I knew I could never go back to her; after the elopement, our relationship was too complicated. I admired and respected Commander Zhu; his daughter looked young and beautiful. She was literate and educated. Marrying her would give me hope for the future.

It was time to move on. With a sigh, I picked up my brush and composed a letter responding to Wang Jianhun. I told him that I was honored and totally in agreement. I gave him the details of my birth date and time and enclosed a photo of myself. Then I added that I would like to get to know this girl before marrying her and wanted to start communicating with her by letter.

In the fall of 1935, our campaign against the Communists came to a halt. The whole 40th Army had a conference for high-ranking officers, and Commander Zhu and Wang Jianhun came to the military headquarters for the meeting. Wang told me privately that the commander's wife, Mrs. Zhu, had hired someone to check out my birthday, and it looked like a good match.

However, she opposed the marriage. "Anybody who has divorced is not reliable," she had told her husband. Also, she was concerned about the age difference, which was seven years. According to the northern Chinese custom, parents preferred arrangements where the man was two or three years younger than the woman. But Commander Zhu said, "Well, my wife doesn't know anything about Yang Ping-Nan. I'm going to make this match work. I'll talk to my wife."

But as for my request to meet his daughter and communicate by letter, he replied firmly, "No. It's not necessary. In our family, with our daughter, we don't do this."

So here I was, a man who believed firmly in the modern concept of love matches, agreeing to an arranged marriage. And yet, oddly, it felt right.

After the meeting, I invited all the high level officers to a dinner. I talked to Commander Zhu privately a little bit. We didn't talk about this marriage. I just asked him, "Is there anything else I should do, Commander Zhu? If there is, please let me know. I'll do everything I can."

He just said, "Well, you don't have to be so polite. We're going to be all in one family now." Then he shook my hand firmly. He kept telling me, "Just take good care of yourself."

In 1936, right after Chinese New Year, Wang Jianhun called me from the regiment headquarters, which was far away from the army headquarters, where I was.

He said, "The deputy commanding general will talk to you today. Whatever he asks you, make sure you agree. Do you hear me?" Then he hung up the phone.

I was a little confused. I didn't know what the deputy commanding general, Ma Fawu, would ask me.

After dinner, Mr. Ma was looking for me. The first thing he said was, "Congratulations! You will have a wife now! I got a call from regiment commander Zhu Jialin. He told me that the marriage of you and his daughter, Bingwen, didn't work out last year. But after the New Year, he sent his assistant, Zhu Yitang, to Baoding with a letter to his wife. In the letter, he scolded his wife and insisted that she drop her opposition to the marriage. After that his wife agreed. Therefore, this matter is settled."

I didn't know what to say, so I didn't say anything.

Then at the end, Ma said, "I also told General Pang about this, and he's happy for you." That was a relief, after the awkwardness about General Pang's daughter.

The next morning, after our early morning meeting, General Pang asked me to have breakfast with him. His breakfast was always shuijiao dumplings. He always ate each dumpling in one bite. After eating a whole bowlful, he asked his assistant, "What's inside the dumplings?"

That morning, he turned around and said to me, "Regiment commander Zhu's daughter is a very good child. I have met her. I already called Mr. Zhang, officer in charge of the Nanyang area. The marriage will be arranged by him. So you don't have to worry about anything. Next month, our troops will be transferred back to Nanyang, and we'll prepare a house for you to stay near the Army headquarters. I'm going to preside over the marriage." Later, he added, "My daughter just got married, in England. What you told my secretary before, about the reason you couldn't marry her, I agree with you."

In the spring of 1936, the 40th Army went back to Nanyang in Henan Province. On April 1st, Bingwen and I were married at the headquarters of the 40th Army, in a building that used to be a general's mansion during the Qing dynasty. Just as he had promised, General Pang presided over the wedding ceremony. We had a big party.

In his speech, General Pang said, "Yang Ping-Nan is a genius. From today, he is going to be Mr. Zhu's son-in-law, and he will also be the 40th Army's son-in-law." There were about 50 tables of guests at the banquet, and the military band provided the music. It was very festive.

The third day after the marriage, General Pang and Commander Zhu, my father-in-law, gave us a large sum of money for us to go to Beijing for a honeymoon. We stayed in a hotel near Qianmen, for thirty days. During the day, we went to Forbidden City, Dongdan, Xidan, Zhongnanhai, Yiheyuan, Yuanmingyuan, Western Hills, and in the evening we went to see the best Beijing opera performances by the most famous singers. We had several photos taken at a studio. We also visited her birthplace and extended family in the village of Weigongcun, in the hills west of Beijing.

Actually, during that month, Feng Zixin's image still came to my mind, from time to time. Once, during dinner, I was thinking, if Feng Zixin had somehow managed to find me when I was stationed in Beijing in 1933, my life might have been totally different.

Bingwen looked at me and asked, "What are you thinking about?"

I said, "I am looking at your eyes."

Still, I felt extremely lucky – not because I saw Feng Zixin's eyes and nose, but because I saw that Bingwen had the kind of tenderness and innocence that Feng Zixin didn't have. This provided me with the foundation of my lifelong happiness, which has been the envy of many people.

After we returned from our honeymoon trip, the army headquarters moved to Xinxiang. We moved into a little house near the train station. We lived a heavenly life together as newlyweds.

Chapter Twenty-Six

THE JAPANESE INVASION

ON DECEMBER 12th of the same year, the Xi'an incident happened. Generalissimo Chiang Kai-Shek, head of the national army and the central government, was tricked into going to Xi'an, where he was arrested and imprisoned by Marshal Zhang Xueliang, former warlord of Manchuria, who wanted him to stop fighting the Communists and join forces to fight against the Japanese invaders. This incident threw the whole country, especially the army, into chaos. No one knew who was in charge.

General Pang asked me to draft and prepare two telegrams: one to Zhang Xueliang and the other to General He Yingqin, who represented Chiang Kai-Shek. Also, I represented him on a visit to Kaifeng to confer with the Eastern Army Corps of Commander Liu Chi. We talked about moving the 40th Army toward Zhengzhou, a major railway intersection.

On December 25th, I also represented General Pang on a journey to Tongguan in Shaanxi Province. When I passed Luoyang, I heard a huge number of firecrackers.

Everywhere the national flag was flying. Then I found out that Chiang Kai-Shek had already left Xi'an to safely return to Nanjing. Immediately I rushed to the National Xigong Military Base in Luoyang to find out what was happening. When I got there, General Pang had just arrived also. Chiang Kai-Shek was back in charge. Together, we returned to Xinxiang that evening.

In February 1937, the 40th Army was moved to Yuncheng in Shanxi Province to try to intercept the Northeast Army, led by Zhang Xueliang, to stop it from crossing the Yellow River.

On April 1st, to celebrate our first wedding anniversary, the 115th regiment commander Liu invited Bingwen and me to visit Jiezhou, a small town near Yuncheng, birthplace of the historical and legendary red-faced general Guan Gong of the Three Kingdoms. We were entertained there. It was very nice. The scenery was stunning.

After the party, we all returned to Yuncheng. Suddenly, Bingwen had a severe stomach ache. It got worse and worse. The chief medical officer of our army came with three other doctors, and they checked her. For the whole evening, they couldn't determine what the problem was. After daybreak, they arranged a military car to take us to another town called Fenglingdu. By noon, we arrived at another place called Weihui, where there was a hospital run by foreigners. A female physician from Norway did an examination and determined that it was a severe inflammation of the bladder. She treated it. After we stayed there three days, Bingwen was fine.

But the female doctor told me, "Your wife's uterus is in the wrong position. She can't bear any children. Do you want me to do surgery on her to correct it?"

I said, "Of course. We would very much like to have a baby." So I signed, and Bingwen was taken to an operating room.

The next day, the doctor told me, "Your wife cannot bear much pain, so the operation was not entirely successful. If you have good luck, maybe within three years, she could have a child. If she hasn't gotten pregnant after three years, it probably won't happen unless she has another operation." This news made me uncomfortable and unhappy.

Then Zhu Yitang came to the hospital, sent by Commander Zhu Jialin, who wanted to know how Bingwen was doing. He was a personal assistant to Zhu Jialin and also a distant relative. Zhu Jialin also sent some money; he was afraid we had spent all our money at the hospital.

After we checked out of the hospital, we returned to Xinxiang. We lived in a relatively large house in Xinxiang. We had two male military assistants at home, and also we found a woman who was a very good cook. So I was running between home in Xinxiang and the army headquarters in Yuncheng.

In June 1937, Zhu Jialin, my father-in-law, was promoted to be the regiment commander of 115th regiment, with the rank of major general. So I went to his headquarters to congratulate him. He asked me to stay overnight. Privately, he told me, "As a commander of a regiment, I am not sure I can do a very good job. My strength is that I am very analytical, and I consider all aspects of an operation. My shortcoming is that I have difficulty making decisions. So I should be a chief of staff for somebody; I really shouldn't be a commander. Please talk to General Pang. The ideal situation for me would be if he made me the chief of staff of the 40th Army. He should appoint someone else to be commander of the regiment. I trust that General Pang will listen to your recommendation."

I couldn't say no; I wouldn't do that. But at the time, General Pang was in Beijing and I was busy with work in my department. So I didn't have a chance to talk to him right away.

Suddenly, on July 7, 1937, the Marco Polo Bridge Incident (Lugouqiao) happened. Japanese troops opened fire on our troops, just outside Beijing. It seemed clear that this was the beginning of the full-scale Japanese invasion of Central China.

I was in Xinxiang. After I heard the news, I immediately sent my wife to Zhangdefu, another town, together with her mother, Zhu Jialin's wife. I thought it was safer for her to stay with her family. Then I immediately went to Shijiazhuang, where I would see both General Pang and Major General Zhu Jialin.

When I arrived at headquarters, I went immediately to meet with General Pang and tactfully explained the desire of my father-in-law, to turn down the promotion. General Pang replied, "If you had told me a little earlier, I would have agreed. But tomorrow is the day when we are going to send all our troops to the front line in Cang-zhou, to fight the Japanese. We expect to face open fire from the Japanese. You cannot ask me to change my generals at this point. When we have a breather, at a later time, I will consider making the change."

That same night, I told my father-in-law about this conversation. He was disappointed. The thought of leading troops into battle filled him with dread.

"This war will last at least five years, maybe longer," he said. "The fighting will be intense. If something happens to me during this time, please make sure you will take care of my family."

At the time, I didn't know what to say, other than to nod my head.

On July 20th, less than two weeks after the Japanese crossed the bridge, our army engaged in its first fire fight with the Japanese. Initially, we took the strategy of setting up a defensive position during the day, then at night going out on offensive actions. Initially, that was very effective. But then the enemy troops started using their air force and heavy equipment, especially tanks. We took heavy casualties, and we started to retreat.

Under the cover of No. 2 and No. 25 regiment, which both had stronger artillery equipment, we managed to retreat to Dezhou. After that, we were able to have a short breather. Unfortunately, the war continued getting worse for us after that.

On my personal front, things also started going badly. Somebody had reported to the Central Command in Nanjing, to the Kuomintang general commissar department, that Yang Ping-Nan could no longer serve in his independent role as a political commissar. They said I should be watching and reporting on the 40th Army's military operations, yet I had married a commander's daughter, which disqualified me to be the head of the commissar department for the 40th Army. I was supposed to be reporting back to Central Command about the activities of General Pang, but it seemed to them that my loyalties might now be with the 40th Army, no longer with Nanjing. Therefore, Central Command sent another person to replace me as chief political commissar of the 40th Army.

They transferred me to the 28th Army, to serve as the head of its political commissar department. When I got the news of that appointment, I immediately went back to Xinxiang to see my wife. At that time, the whole Zhu family had already moved back to Xinxiang. I found out that the 28th Army was in Hunan Province, in the town of Pingxiang, recuperating and resupplying. They were not planning on moving soon. Therefore, I needed to go there immediately to take up my new assignment. Bingwen insisted she go with me to Pingxiang.

We took the train to Changsha in Hunan Province. There I checked in at the 28th Army representative office. We found out that the Japanese army was attacking Shanghai, and fighting in Shanghai was getting very intense. The 28th Army was given the order to provide assistance to the Shanghai campaign.

So I had to immediately take Bingwen back to Hankou. I managed to call my mother-in-law to tell her she was coming. I put her on the next train north on the Ping-Han line, which ran from Beijing to Hankou.

By then we knew what we had suspected earlier: Bingwen was with child. It seemed so cruel to put this small, young woman, pregnant, on a train, alone, in the midst of this terrible war. We never knew what rail lines might be blown up or taken over by the Japanese army. Plus, I was being sent into a war zone, to defend Shanghai.

At the Dazhimen train station in Hankou, we held each other and cried and cried. It felt like this was our last moment together.

Chapter Twenty-Seven

INTO BATTLE

DEVASTATED, I TURNED around and returned to Changsha, where I changed trains and went to Hangzhou to join the 28th Army. The day I got there was mid-autumn festival. The top commander of the 28th Army was another Mr. Zhu, a big fat guy from Hunan. He invited me to a Moon Festival dinner. I remember he gave me a big piece of fish. He said, "This is the famous West Lake vinegar fish. Please eat more."

That same night, I wrote a long letter to Bingwen, writing almost until daybreak. The next morning, after eating breakfast, I got on the train and went to Shanghai. A low-level assistant had been assigned to me as head of the commissar department. Talking to him, I found out that he was a classmate of mine at the military academy. He was a graduate of Henan University, yet here he was, reporting to me. It is really hard to predict people's fates.

That afternoon, the day I arrived in Shanghai, our army got involved in a fire fight in the Jiangwan campaign. We were under the overall command of a very famous general called Zhang Fakui. He was one of the main generals under Chiang Kai-Shek. We stayed mostly in people's homes, but none of the houses was occupied. All the people had fled.

Every day, the fighting became fiercer. The enemy started air raids. There was no time for warning, and there were no air raid shelters. Sometimes, our only option was to take cover in the nearby cotton fields. One time, I was eating lunch and suddenly we heard the sound of an enemy airplane. My bodyguard dragged me into the cotton field.

As soon as we hid ourselves on the ground under the plants, machine-gun fire strafed over us. My body-guard was shot in the head and died instantly. My cap had a bullet hole in it. That's how close I came to dying that day.

For the following several days, we were just dodging Japanese air raids. There was no way for our army to fight back. I often found time to write letters to Bingwen. I tried to call several times but could not get through. It was frustrating in the extreme. I didn't even know if she had made it back to her family safely.

One day, fat General Zhu asked me to go to his office to see him. He said, "In our army, most of the soldiers are new recruits. A lot of them have run away. As the army's political commissar, is there anything you can do to stop this?"

I said, "I have only about a hundred people under my command. We cannot watch all the new soldiers to prevent them from running away. There's nothing we can do."

He shook his head. Then his assistant walked in and said, "General, your chief of staff was just killed."

After that, I just walked away. It seemed we were all powerless to do anything in the face of this horrible invasion.

The city of Shanghai was in panic and chaos. Everybody knew the battle was lost. General Zhu ordered me to go to Songjiang, another part of Shanghai, and try to contact the local government, in order to arrange for a retreat.

It so happened that when I set out for Songjiang on the following day, the bridge connecting Songjiang and Shanghai was destroyed by the Japanese army. So I could not get to Songjiang to fulfill my orders. I immediately called the office of the general chief commissar in Nanjing and explained the situation to them.

After that, I got on the train to return to Hangzhou. From the radio, I heard that Shanghai had already been taken over by the Japanese. It seemed our army had disintegrated. I was really scared. It was every man for himself.

All I could think was: I have to get back to Bingwen. I couldn't protect Shanghai, but perhaps I could protect my wife. What if Japanese troops took over the town where she was staying? Now that the 28th Army had fallen apart, my place was with her.

So I got on another train, to Jiujiang in Jiangxi. There, I waited for two days. I managed to get on a British boat heading up the Yangtze River. I got off the boat in Hankou. The first thing I did was go to the Dazhimen train station, where I last saw my wife. In my heart, I was thinking, if I never saw her again, she would set up a mark here, always looking for her husband on that spot.

On the following day, I got on the Ping-Han train, going north. When the train arrived in Zhengzhou, I discovered that I was the only one in the first class car. I asked the conductor, "Which is your next stop?"

He said, "Temporarily, I think we are going to have to stop at Zhangde, because Shijiazhuang is already lost. I cannot predict anything." I was really very scared.

When the train arrived in Xinxiang, I got out at that station. I ran into a man I knew. He said, "All the 40th Army people have gone. What are you doing here?"

So I called a rickshaw and went directly to the home of Zhu Jialin's family. The landlord saw me and said, "Amazing. You're here! Your wife's eyes almost went blind with crying. Your mother-in-law kept saying you shouldn't have gone to Shanghai. Two days ago, they all moved to Weinan."

When he said this, he opened up his drawer and took out an address in Weinan. When I returned to the train station, I was lucky to get on a train that belonged to the 32nd Army, heading south. That same night, I arrived in Zhengzhou, where I changed trains to go west to Weinan.

At about midnight, I arrived in Weinan. The landlord must have called or sent a telegram, because Bingwen was waiting for me at the train station. From a distance, I could see her long hair, flowing in the autumn wind. We saw each other, almost like we were from different worlds. We held each other tightly, and I could feel the firm bump of her belly. Both of us were smiling, but our eyes were covered with tears. We could not say a word.

I vowed that we would never be separated again.

Chapter Twenty-Eight

MID-WINTER BIRTH

WHEN I HAD LEFT the 40th Army, I took with me some really beautiful memories. My only regret was that I did not manage to fulfill my father-in-law's wishes of getting his job changed.

In Weinan, I found out what had happened to the 40th Army during my absence. In the battle for Cangzhou, they suffered huge losses and damage. When they got to Dezhou, they regrouped; some of the injured soldiers were sent to Haizhou, near my hometown, for treatment. Later, I found out that my father-in-law had sent one of his assistants to visit my parents and check out my background. They found out that I had a daughter from my previous marriage, but by then Huiling's mother had died.

After reuniting with Bingwen, I received a new assignment, one that was safer and more stable. It was as a political instructor at the Luoyang branch of the Whampoa Military Academy, with the title of lieutenant colonel (zhongxiao). Under the then-regulations, when people were assigned to the military academy, they were always demoted one level, but their salary was not affected.

As soon as I was hired, Bingwen and I had to rush to Luoyang, even though she was getting close to her delivery date. I had heard that there was a chance the military academy might be moved away from Luoyang to a more secure location.

Our train arrived in Luoyang on a snowy day in the late afternoon, on a winter day near the end of the Chinese year. Bingwen started to have unbearable pains when we were still on the train.

As soon as we got off the train, I had to rush out to look for a hospital. I found a Catholic mission hospital close to the train station, run by European priests. At that hospital, they treated mainly wounded soldiers. Initially they said they would not accept a woman for childbirth. But I took her there anyway, and when they saw her, they agreed.

There was a nurse and with the help of a doctor, after six hours of screaming and pain, with a lot of sweat and tears, Bingwen gave birth to a healthy baby boy. The birth was so difficult that afterwards, she was almost in shock. So that's why it's known in China that your birthday is also your mother's day of suffering.

Our son, Yang Bao, was born on the 25ᵗʰ day of the Twelfth Month, according to the Chinese calendar. This was five days before the Chinese New Year, sometimes called Spring Festival, so my mother-in-law wanted to give him the name Yang Chun, which means 'spring.' I didn't like the name Yang Chun, so I changed it to Yang Bao. Later, when my son entered school, I gave him the more formal name of Yang Jeon Chao. Even later, when he went to America, he chose the English name Paul, because it sounds like Bao.

I reported to work at the military academy as soon as I could. The head of the commissar department of Luoyang academy, Mr. Lin, took an immediate disliking toward me. He was openly hostile, and every day I worried that he would fire me. So I had to be patient and bow my head in humility just to keep my job.

Just a few weeks later, on the 15th day after Chinese New Year, the academy notified all the families to be prepared to move to Hanzhong, in southwestern Shaanxi Province. The war was getting more intense, and the fighting was too close to Luoyang, which was on a major rail line. Hanzhong was in a distant mountainous area, less likely to be attacked by the Japanese.

At that time, Yang Bao was not even one month old. All the other instructors were ordered to leave with their families, except me. Mr. Lin deliberately ordered me to stay. I went to Mr. Lin and asked him that I be permitted to leave with my family. He said, "No. If you want to leave with your family, you might as well resign." He disliked me very much and was trying to get rid of me.

So my Bingwen had to leave with our tiny baby and travel west with the rest of the families. I had promised never to leave her again. After she left, I lost my bearings. Every day, I worried. I had no way of knowing how they were doing.

Later on, I found out, Bingwen had a terribly hard time during that journey. The group of families got off the train in Baoji, but they could not get a hotel room, so she had to stay in the entrance hall of the hotel, huddling with the tiny baby, and use her suitcase to shield against the winter wind. After another wife saw Bingwen with a baby, she offered to let her come into her hotel room and sleep on her floor.

After a few days, Bingwen and the baby got on a military truck to Hanzhong, traveling with the other academy families. When they were going over the Qinling mountains, the truck broke down. It was snowing heavily and a strong wind was blowing, and they didn't know what to do. They were not near a village or a town, and it was bitter cold in the back of the truck. Finally, all the families together got off the truck and walked. Bing-wen, who had given birth less than a month earlier, had to carry our tiny baby through the snowy mountains, at an altitude of about 1800 meters or 6,000 feet. One man, named Mr. Du, was walking with his wife and a baby, too, and he helped my wife. Finally they managed to get over the mountain and find a hotel.

Three months later, I was allowed to go to Hanzhong to join Bingwen and our baby, Yang Bao. What a tough start he got in his life.

Chapter Twenty-Nine

SAFE HAVEN

AFTER I ARRIVED in Hanzhong, we moved to Wuxiangzhen, a small village about 30 kilometers from Hanzhong. The Chinese currency was losing its value. Our lives were getting harder all the time.

The war was going badly; we kept losing battles. That year, the fighting was especially fierce in southern Shandong and northern Jiangsu. The 40th army casualties were very substantial. The dead and injured totaled almost 60% of the whole army.

In July, we received terrible news about Zhu Jialin. He died during the battle at Huishanhu near Taier-zhuang in April 1938. His troops were defeated and surrounded by the Japanese; he shot himself rather than surrender and be taken as a prisoner of war. To this day, every time we go to the Taipei Martyr's Shrine, to visit his memorial, I always feel a deep sense of regret. If I had not left the 40th Army, during those months I could have most likely fulfilled Zhu Jialin's wish, to get him transferred to a staff job.

Bingwen also felt terribly hurt and sad. I quickly made arrangements so that the whole Zhu family could come to live with us in Hanzhong. This included Zhu Jialin's wife, his son, two daughters, and the nanny of the youngest daughter. I never forgot that I had promised Zhu Jialin to care for his entire family if anything should happen to him. I did my best to keep this promise.

Eventually, my boss, Mr. Lin, changed his treatment of me by 180 degrees. First, Zhu Xiaozhou, the head of the academy and also the military commander of that whole region, started a monthly publication. He asked Mr. Lin to be the editor. Every instructor of the academy had to submit some articles for this publication. The articles had to do with contemporary affairs, military conditions, and the political situation. In the first issue, I had two articles. After this, I was expected to submit at least two articles for every issue. Some of these articles were reprinted in newspapers around the country, and Mr. Lin was very pleased.

Another time, when I was giving a lecture about the military confrontation between the Chu and Han kingdoms and analyzing their geopolitical conditions during the Han Dynasty, it happened that Bai Chongxi, the Defense Minister of China, happened to come into my classroom and listen to my lecture. Afterwards, he gave me an award; this made the whole academy look good.

At the same time, Northwestern University asked Mr. Lin to recommend an instructor to give lectures there about contemporary affairs. That college was in a city called Cheng-gu, about 100 Chinese miles away from the military academy. They wanted someone who could give a lecture every Monday morning, to all the students and faculty, about the current war situation, followed by a two-hour class on politics in the afternoon. Mr. Lin, without any hesitation, recommended me for the job.

So I started a second job, teaching at Northwestern University. Teaching there gave me a great sense of satisfaction. First, I was lecturing at a university even though I never went to college myself. Second, I got more pay and therefore we had a better life. We could eat better. Sometimes I would bring home cookies or meat or other special food for my wife and mother-in-law. Third, I made sure that Zhu Bingyan, the only son of Zhu Jialin, went to the high school associated with Northwestern University. Later he went to college at Northwestern and studied mechanical engineering. That made me very happy because I promised Zhu Jialin I would take care of his family.

The biggest joy in my life was our little son. Normally, little children prefer to stick close to their mother. I was like that when I was in elementary school. But Yang Bao was different. When he was little, he was like a postage stamp, always sticking close to me. After his mother stopped nursing him, he started to sleep snuggled up with me.

During the day, I was very busy. I had to go to the military academy to teach and also to Northwestern University, and often I wrote articles for publication. Still, I always managed to make some time to play with him. Often I took him to the rocky river side, and we played with the rocks there. Today, when I pass a department store in Taipei and see a lot of toys in the window, I feel sorry that when my son was young, I didn't have enough money to buy him toys. I only played with him in the sand, with rocks.

Little Yang Bao not only started to run, he could say a lot of words. He always had a lot of questions. Sometimes I found this frustrating! For instance, one day we took him out and he noticed a shop selling fabric. He asked, "What is this?" I answered, "Fabric." He asked, "What is fabric for?" I answered, "To make clothes." He asked, "Why do you want to make clothes?" I didn't know how to answer that one!

During those years, Bingwen often had stomach aches. One time, my mother-in-law said, "This time it's not a stomach problem. She's pregnant again." I was very happy, but I knew this was a tough time to bring another baby into the world. At that time, we were so poor that sometimes we didn't even have enough money to buy rice.

Late that summer, our daughter, Yang Luo, was born. My mother-in-law often scolded us, saying, "The Japanese are fighting so close to us, and you two keep having babies. What are you doing?"

The life we had in those few years in Wuxiangzhen was tough. My whole family, the four of us, slept on one bed, made of bamboo, which had only three legs. To replace the fourth leg, we had to place a stool underneath it to keep it stable. Our whole bathroom consisted of a bucket with sand in it and a used wine barrel, instead of a toilet. We took them out once a day to clean.

In 1941, Northwestern University moved to Lanzhou, so I had to give up that second job. But Bingwen started to teach at the Wuxiangzhen Elementary School. She was paid not in money but in rice. Her salary was five bushels of rice. So during those terrible war years, we all had enough rice to eat, including my in-laws. My salary was getting higher and higher but it was worth less and less. After 1942, a big bundle of cash could not even buy a bottle of soy sauce.

The famous Chinese saying, "Heaven never bars one's way," means "Don't despair; there's always a way out." In February of 1943, Mr. Zhu Xiaozhou, the head of the military academy in Hanzhong, was appointed by Chiang Kai-Shek to be governor of Shaanxi Province. Among the instructors at the military academy, I was the only person he selected to go with him to Xi'an, to serve as his personal secretary. This was an honor and a great opportunity for me.

After I arrived in Xi'an, when he assumed his position as governor, I prepared his first speech to the people of Shaanxi Province. I also prepared a news release to present at a press conference. The public reaction was very positive.

Soon after that, he appointed me to be executive director of the provincial price control commission. That job had a lot of authority, in charge of controlling prices in the whole province.

At the end of April, the Japanese crossed the Yellow River in Henan. Many refugees came flooding through Zijing Pass toward Xi'an. One day, the wife of Chou Peisheng came to me. Seeing her ugly face vividly reminded me of the forty silver dollars they had taken from me when I had nothing. She said, "My husband was killed during a recent battle against the Japanese. I have nowhere to go now. I hope you will forgive us for what we did to you in the past. I hope you will help me."

"I'm not going to remember what you did to me," I said, "but I cannot take you into my home. So leave now."

A few days later, my friend Lu Deju arrived in Xi'an. He came with his whole family, about ten people, including his father and brothers, all very poor. I arranged for new clothes and a haircut for all of them and invited them to a big meal at a restaurant. After that, I took Lu Deju to Lianhu Park, and we talked a long time.

"From now on," I told him, "as long as I have something to eat, you don't ever have to worry again."

He told me that Feng Shujing, after marrying a military officer, had died in an air raid in Hankou. As it happens, the Japanese army never stationed troops in my hometown of Nancheng. Under Japanese rule, Xinghua, where I escaped with Feng Shujing and stayed in a small hotel, became the temporary capital of Jiangsu Province.

On the following day, I gave Lu Deju a job in my office. I also found jobs for his relatives and a place for them all to live.

In March of 1944, I was appointed as the county executive of Baoji. At that time, Baoji was the biggest county in Shaanxi province. It was a very important transportation hub for the whole region behind the enemy lines, connecting Xi'an with the wartime capital in Chongqing. It was in the western part of the province, at the junction of two major rail lines. Lu Deju's father came with me to Baoji and worked in the county educational department.

In the winter of 1944, after I had started my job as county executive of Baoji, I went to Xi'an to attend a conference called by the governor for all the county executives of the province. The county executive from a remote northern county called Luochuan, a man named Mr. Hu, came and looked for me at the beginning of the conference. He asked for me to meet with him privately. So we made an appointment to have lunch together at the Xijing Hotel.

Over lunch, Mr. Hu told me that Feng Zixin asked him to send her regards. It turned out that Feng Zixin and her husband, a man named Li, both worked for the Kuomintang Party office of Luochuan county. She saw my name in one of the newspapers and she knew that I would probably be at this conference.

Mr. Hu gave me a letter from Feng Zixin. I grabbed it and read it immediately. She wrote:

"All these years I have been living in a surreal otherworld. Last year, I somehow ended up in Luochuan. In a confused state of mind, I married Mr. Li Wenjing. After we were married, we often quarreled. But after tomorrow, I don't think we will quarrel anymore because we have filed for divorce. If you ask me what I am going to do in the future, my answer is a blank. I never tried to write to you because I could not bring myself to write a single word. I don't really wish to receive a letter from you because that would be 'unnecessary.' I understand. From now on, life will go on. It's possible that someday we may bump into each other on a train."

My hands shook as I read it, and I had to look away. Luochuan was about 200 kilometers north of Xi'an, close to Yan'an, the area occupied by the Communists.

Mr. Hu said that when Feng Zixin gave him the note, she appeared to be very sad, almost in tears. So I asked Mr. Hu if he knew anything about my relationship with Feng Zixin. He said, "I have heard a little bit."

I said to Mr. Hu, "Please tell her I am doing fine here. But I can never forget her. She will never be out of my thoughts. I hope someday I will see her on a train."

After that day, every time I got on a train, I began to subconsciously look around among the other passengers, wishing that one of them might be Feng Zixin.

Chapter Thirty

AFTER THE WAR

ONE SUMMER DAY in 1945, we were watching a Chinese opera in a large concert hall in Baoji. Suddenly we heard the sound of firecrackers and gunfire. We heard people screaming, "The Japanese devils have surrendered! The war is over!" Everything was in chaos. The police protected me and escorted us out of the theater.

The next day, we held a big victory celebration. More than 100,000 people took part in a huge parade in the streets of Baoji. After that, we also had a special party, inviting all the local American Air Force officers and their families. It was a joyful and festive occasion. A lot of local men sat on top of trucks or cars and shot their pistols into the sky.

For the next couple months, we were very busy. Baoji was a major hub for train and bus and air transportation. Almost every day, high level officials came to visit me. Only one person in my office could speak English, so we had to occasionally invite a local dentist, who spoke reasonably good English, to help translate.

Yang Bao remembered this dentist because he pulled several of his teeth. Each time, he was so scared that Huang Fuguang, my body guard, had to catch him and wrestle him to the ground to get him to the dental chair.

In the fall of 1946, security conditions in Shaanxi Province were deteriorating because of the civil war with the Communists. Governor Zhu consolidated many military organizations under his command and became the commander in chief. At that time, he had one military chief of staff and one executive chief of staff, both with the rank of major general. I was selected to be executive chief of staff for Governor Zhu.

During the two and a half years I worked in Baoji, I set two records. I was the youngest chief executive of Baoji, ever. Also, I was considered the most honest and clean, uncorrupt. I had a reputation for always being very conscientious. I received several awards. So when I was leaving, I was given many honors by the provincial government. Even the U.S. Air Force gave me an official recognition. Many local business leaders and other people held farewell parties.

After the train left Baoji, when it arrived at one major village, ten older gentlemen representing various local districts came to meet me. They jointly brought me a pail of clear water and a large mirror. That symbolized that during my administration, everything was 'clear like water and bright like a mirror.' The next day, many of the major papers in the province and even some papers in Nanjing ran articles about this. That was one of the proudest moments of my professional life.

When I returned to Xi'an, I also brought Lu Deju's father and the rest of his family back to Xi'an. I arranged a new job for Lu Deju, although it was still low level. Because he was only a high school graduate, I could not arrange a higher position for him. However he was able to live a pretty comfortable life with that job. In 1947, when I moved my family from Xi'an to Nanjing, I specifically asked the head of personnel in our office, Mr. Wu, to make sure to take good care of Lu Deju and his family.

When I reported to my new assignment at the Shaanxi Provincial government, I found out my responsibility was huge—more than ten times what my responsibility had been as Baoji county executive. The commander-in-chief, the governor, didn't really do much in that office, nor did the deputy commander-in-chief. The military chief of staff had responsibility only for military matters. So all other matters regarding the governance of the province came under my jurisdiction. Governor Zhu basically gave me full authority for the operation of the whole province, including the security of the provincial government offices. The governor's office was located in a compound inside the former imperial palace built during the Tang Dynasty.

During our first meeting, the governor made clear certain understandings. For any personnel matters involving military personnel at the rank of captain or below, all decisions would be up to me. As far as the budget, anything below one million yuan would be my responsibility. Any criminal or legal matters involving any penalties other than the death sentence were my responsibility; I would make the final decisions. So I was very nervous when I first took over the job.

In the fall of 1947, because Baoji was briefly occupied by Communist forces, the county executive officers of Baoji all disappeared. That made Chiang Kai-Shek very angry. In a meeting in Nanjing, governor Zhu was given an in-your-face tongue-lashing. He was told he should prepare to leave his post within three months. With that knowledge, in January 1948, I resigned and took my family back to Nanjing. We lived with Mr. Wu Youxia, an old friend from Haizhou, one of my brightest students in the normal school. The Wu family had a large house and shared it with us.

When we moved to Nanjing, we took with us a lot of typical Northwestern products, including fur clothing and Chinese medicine. I immediately began to visit some old friends and relatives in Nanjing, looking for my next job. I took one fur coat to Santaiye, my grandfather's younger brother. My heart was troubled when I went to see him. He was the one who originally said he was going to send me to the Yang Family shrine to be punished for eloping with Feng Shujing when I was young. But he was very happy to see me. He insisted I stay for dinner.

After a few drinks of strong clear liquor, he began to talk. "Starting in the Qing dynasty, our county in Haizhou has had only three people who became county executives. All three of them were named Yang," he told me. "One served during the Daoguang period of the Qing dynasty as county executive in Laizhou, Shandong Province."

The second one was Santaiye himself. "After the Northern Expedition, the President's office asked me to be the county executive of Funing County, Jiangsu Province. But only about five months later, the warlord Sun Chuanfang sent his army over and took over Funing, and I had to flee. I almost lost my life.

"You are the third. We did not expect that you would do such a good job over there. We saw reports of your work fairly frequently. Under the traditions followed during the Qing dynasty, normally when any local man received this kind of honor, the emperor would sign a plaque for you to display in your home."

After I left Santaiye's home, it was raining a little, and I felt chilled. Subconsciously, I walked to No. 1 Park, where fifteen years earlier, in 1933, Feng Zixin and I spent the whole night together, holding on to each other, saying good-bye. All the scenery and pagodas were still the same, but the people had changed.

As Du Fu stated in his poem: 'She probably has married and has a big family with a lot of children.' I wish her well forever.

EPILOGUE

IN MAY of 1949, our small family of four moved from Shanghai to Taiwan. We managed to get tickets on two of the last flights out before the Communists took over the airport. In Taipei, we lived at first in a Japanese-style house on Nanchang Street.

That same month, on May 25th, Shanghai was lost to the Communists. From Taiwan, I listened to the radio broadcast every day to find out what was happening.

It was probably on the 28th or 29th of May that I heard an announcement from a Shanghai radio station, saying that a group of 'counter-revolutionaries' had been executed. Among them, they mentioned the name of Lu Deju. They identified him as a native of Lianyungang. I was heart-stricken and horrified! Lu Deju was truly a friend in the classical, romantic sense. I will remember him fondly for the rest of my life.

As for Feng Zixin, I never saw her again. The county where she was last living, Luochuan, was only sixty miles from Yan'an, wartime headquarters of the Communist Party. At first I assumed that the Communists must have killed her, since she worked for the Nationalist Party.

Recently, though, I have begun to imagine another life for her. Perhaps, after she left her husband, in that confused state, she ran off to Yan'an and joined the Communists. She was always romantic and idealistic; their high-minded pronouncements appealed to many educated young people. As a nurse, her skills would have been valuable to them. Perhaps she found a sense of purpose with them. Perhaps they honor her today as an early revolutionary.

Or perhaps she, too, escaped to Taiwan.

I still look for her, subconsciously, every time I board a train.

THE END

Manufactured by Amazon.ca
Bolton, ON